Wilt Thou Be Made Whole?

GEORG KÜHLEWIND

Wilt Thou Be Made Whole?

Healings in The Gospels

TRANSLATED AND INTRODUCED BY

Michael Lipson, Ph.D.

LINDISFARNE BOOKS
2008

Wilt Thou Be Made Whole? is translated by Michael Lipson, Ph.D. It was originally published in German as *Gesunden im Licht: Die Heilungen in den Evangelien* by Verlag Freies Geistesleben, Stuttgart, Germany, 2004.

Published by Lindisfarne Books
610 Main Street, Great Barrington, Massachusetts 01230
www.lindisfarne.org

Library of Congress Cataloging-in-Publication Data is available.

Printed in the United States

CONTENTS

Introduction
by Michael Lipson, Ph.D   7

Preface   13
How to read this book   14
Orientation   14

Foreword   17

  I. Psychosomatics   21

  II. The Anthroposophical Basis of Healings
    in the Language of the New Testament   37

III. The "Psychiatric" Healings   51

IV. Bodily Healings   63

  V. Gospel Healings in the Light
    of Anthroposophy   95

Appendices   105

Notes   115

Further Reading   119

INTRODUCTON

"BEWARE WHEN THE GREAT GOD lets loose a thinker on this planet," wrote Emerson. He might almost have been speaking of Georg Kühlewind (1924–2006), the Hungarian chemist, linguist, philosopher and mystic who shocked heavenward all those fortunate enough to meet him.

There was always something a bit dangerous about Georg's presence. It was not ill will: no one could be more compassionate. It was not a dark mood: no one could have a lighter wit, even in the face of horror. It was nothing unbalanced: no one could draw on healthier psychic roots. Yet there was a sense of things on the move, of discoveries that might take you who knows where, of having to put down your baggage and for once run free. Freedom: that was the danger in Georg's presence, threatening to everything in us that wants stasis and self-protection. It included a great sense of liveliness, like pure oxygen, and this miraculous spaciousness occurred even in the simplest of conversations. As Georg's beloved poet Rainer Maria Rilke wrote,

See, I live. But from what?
Neither childhood nor future are diminished:
Existence, past all reckoning, springs forth in my
heart.

Georg had a *look*, a glance, a way of communicating intensely with his eyes, that conveyed a special flavor of intelligent love. This glance was an expression of his total concern for everyone in the meditation groups he taught. When someone was missing from the group after a break, for instance, he always knew who it was, even in a group of 80 people he'd just met. Listening to the often cloudy meditation reports by participants, he would fasten on just the gem, the light, and refer to it later in the midst of his teaching. His own meditation reports opened the theme to us, always from a different angle, and with a different intensity, than we expected. Though the theme had seemed abstract and theoretical, his report could demonstrate a devotional, loving aspect we had not imagined.

When participants reported on their meditation with quotations or old thoughts, Georg would occasionally meet their contribution with a searching, "Do you *know* that?" For despite his scholarly approach to literature, music, linguistics, psychology and epistemology, Georg's orientation toward spiritual worlds was experiential from start to finish. His own books are the account of what he himself experienced; they are not musings, or conglomerations of the insights of others. When asked about matters of karma or cosmic history of which he had no direct meditative experience, he was happy often to say he just didn't know. Georg called himself an "empirical idealist": that is, someone who lives in a world comprised entirely of meaning and makers of meaning.

In speaking of spiritual or personal matters, Georg was often moved to tears. He had lived through two Nazi death-camps as a youth, and suffered many losses and confusions of fate throughout his life. Perhaps, along with his spiritual work, these events had opened his heart. The impression he gave, however, was of being able to bear tremendous intensities of feeling *before* giving way to tears. And he could switch back, in a breath, from the overwhelm of feeling to a fresh, crystal-clear exploration of the subject at hand. He said, "We have tears, sometimes of sorrow, sometimes of joy, but then: back to the theme! That is always the gesture." The whole spiritual path, for Georg, is there in our fundamental capacity to concentrate. To hear him teach was to be aware that this capacity can be deepened to a fantastic degree. It enabled him to listen more intimately to the world, so uncovering whole new ranges of experience, as when he reported on a meditation that he was reluctant to put into words, that was not originally in words, but that he formulated like this: "To be addressed by someone gives existence. Every moment, Christ is in my heart, whispering, 'YOU ARE'."

Despite his gifts to thousands all over the world, Georg did not claim to be a "good" man, and sometimes explicitly denied that he was one. Yet he said, "The only consequent life is the life of a saint." He tended to the radical formulation, thinking each thought all the way to its end and beyond. When, in this book, he raises the question of whether human beings are born to die, he means it quite literally. In one of our last meetings, I asked him if he thought that really, through our spiritual work, we would one day, perhaps after many incarnations, be able to live in one body without laying it down to death. With complete seriousness, he said he did indeed think so. I asked for examples, and he came up with several, notably the legend of the Indian sage Bodhidharma, founder of Zen and a favorite of Georg's. According to the story, after Bodhidharma's death in China in about 540 AD, one of his disciples met him walking back toward India, barefoot but carrying one sandal on a stick over his shoulder. The disciple rushed to Bodhidharma's tomb, dug it up, and found it empty— except for the other sandal, which he'd left behind in his haste to emerge from the grave. Those of us who love Georg are probably willing now for him to progress through purely spiritual forms. Still, we would be delighted, if not entirely surprised, someday to find him walking in the Vienna woods, carrying one sandal, whistling silently, or clapping with one hand.

What if, as Georg suggests, the world were not meaningless, but vitally important? What if you had a mission, a mission urgent and vast enough to drive you into and through a whole human existence? It's worth considering, since this is the message of the New Testament and especially of the "miraculous" healings explored in this deeply exciting book.

In Georg's view, the healings are neither histories nor symbols. Rather, they are reports of events as *meditations*. This means that we can only approach them through a radically different kind of consciousness, an altogether new intensity of understanding. We miss everything if we read them as accounts of magic, or as supports to religious belief, or as literature.

The Prologue to the Gospel of Saint John, in words Georg said we almost "cannot take seriously enough," claims that creation originally "was life in Him, and the life was the light of human beings." Divine *life*, which creates the world, is also the *light* of human understanding in its original force. The same life, re-creating, became the substance of Jesus' healings and can now become our understanding of them. This means that there cannot be a meditative reading of the healings that does not heal the reader.

Along the way Georg shows that expressions such as "glory," "faith," "life" "power" and "word" are anything but the Sunday-school window-dressing, the spiritual garnish, they can seem to be to our cliché-worn eyes. Instead, as in his earlier *Becoming Aware of the Logos*, he explains them as terms of art, referring to specific spiritual processes that can make an immediate difference in the structure of our own minds. To work our way into their full benefit, such terms must become for us something like musical scores to a musician: in living them out, performing them, we realize what they are all about.

Georg gives us an entire spiritual psychology in these pages. Its cogency, however, depends on our going through, with some energy, the "ponderings" and meditations he offers in each section of the text. To do this, it can be helpful to work with a friend or two. One enlivening way to approach a meditation is first to deny it, to argue against it, and then, releasing this intentional refusal, to find your way into a more intimate affirmation.

The healing direction of the texts takes us into a realm of non-duality, back from the sick individualism by which we cut ourselves off from the Source. Healing re-connects what the Fall split apart: the human and the divine. But our normal, body-oriented consciousness simply cannot take the intensity of non-dual experience of the divine. This is why the shepherds, for example, are afraid of the angelic host (Luke 2:9). To endure the light, to "bear the beams of love," as Blake put it, we can awaken as I AM or the true self. Once we have learned this unusual strength of being, we also turn out to be strong enough to put aside the anxious sheath that separates us, and we can merge playfully with the very heart of the world.

All of this can seem *too good to be true*. We have forgotten that such things are possible. We have a hard time imagining them. We have long since stopped hoping for them. It can seem that to achieve the re-ordering of the universe that Georg describes is simply beyond us. And so it is! For the realm of healing is not to be *achieved* at all, but rather approached through moments of wonder and awe, the way innocent Parzival stumbled upon the Sacred Mountain. Nor does it exist for "us," for the self-pointing, selfish self, but instead healing arises in our forgotten, silent, innermost and most unconsciously familiar self. If you are ready for the Great Adventure, Georg will lead you with a sure step through the brambles of terminology, up the foothills of insight, and suddenly out over an astonishing vista.

Michael Lipson, Ph.D.

PREFACE

EVERY HUMAN, and in fact every being, is a mystery. This means that we cannot understand them through a discursive thinking that moves from concept to concept. A being can only be understood through intuition, a flash of enlightenment, or meditation. The relationship between two beings requires an even higher capacity in non-dualistic knowing and perception. It would be a great illusion, then, to think that the healings in the New Testament can be understood by means of our everyday, word-based thinking. This short book intends to prepare the way, instead, for meditation on these healings, and perhaps to assist in the phase that I call "pondering," which precedes meditation. The book offers handholds and footholds, with which, at least, verbal difficulties can be overcome, thus enabling you to immerse yourself properly in the stories of healing.

How to Read this Book

You will find three distinct thematic lines here: fundamentals of anthropology, fundamentals of the language of the New Testament, and descriptions of the healings with explanations appropriate for meditation. Each healing must be meditated, since, as we shall see, each one has always been inaccessible to everyday consciousness. This is why they are called "miracles."

You can find instructions in meditation in many of my books, for example *Freedom and Light* or *The Soft Will*. In this book the meditations and "ponderings" are meant both as aids in understanding the process of healing and as examples for practicing meditation on the healings.

Orientation

The Gospels are not simply factual reports about events having to do with Jesus. Instead, the authors meditatively "see," or experience, earthly facts that simultaneously represent symbolic images. What the authors experience in this way is then preserved in their writings. Both the meditative experience and the way it is brought down into language result in (mostly slight) variations between the texts, as if someone viewed something from a different angle, perhaps through a different veil.

This state of affairs determines our method of research. After pondering them, the scenes described are then to be meditated as symbolic images. In pondering, we try inwardly to paint for ourselves, very exactly—through a kind of concentrated thinking and mental-picturing—both what is being communicated and what is being left out of the texts. In meditating, these imagistic *events* (for they are nearly always given as a process, only rarely as a static image), are to be taken as the sign for a meaning that cannot be otherwise expressed, and we try to understand this meaning through *signless* (wordless) thinking-feeling-willing.

The Gospels treat the stories of healing with a special tone of respect. When the Lord heals, it is not simply an interpersonal event. It has to do with the very meaning of our existence. To begin to understand these processes, we can use meditation on the one hand, and on the other, any experience we may have with today's "open" human beings who are not as shielded and separated from the spiritual world and from their fellows as are most of us (see Chapter I.2). We find sure signs of the Lord's non-separation in descriptions of how He knew what was going on in the souls of others:

> And Jesus knowing their thoughts said, Wherefore think ye evil in your hearts? For whether is easier, to say, Thy sins be forgiven thee; or to say, Arise, and walk? (Matthew 9:4)

> And Jesus knew their thoughts and said unto them, Every kingdom divided against itself is brought to desolation...(Matthew 12:25) (See also Matthew 16:8; Mark 2:8; Luke 5:22, 6:8, 7:39-40; 9:47, 11:17; John 2:25, 6:61, 6:64)

Openness toward the souls of other human beings is, at the same time, openness toward the spiritual world. The New Testament speaks of the openness of the heavens at the time of Jesus' baptism:

> And Jesus, when he was baptized, went straight-way out of the water: and, lo, the heavens were opened unto him, and he saw the Spirit of God descending like a dove, and lighting upon him... (Matthew 3:16) (See also Mark 1:10, Luke 3:21; John 1:51).

Yet the heavens are always open; it is only we who can be *not open*. Openness means, for us, the possibility of receiving an intuition, a new idea. For someone who is completely open, this would be an ongoing state. God's creative power, the Logos, comes to dwell within him:

> And the Word was made flesh, and dwelt among us (and we beheld his glory, the glory as of the only begotten of the Father) full of grace and truth. (John 1:14)

And this gives Jesus the power (*dynamis*) to heal.

The healings occur when, at least for a moment, the consciousness of the sick person (or his or her representative) is raised into the *superconscious* where there are no forms, and where the *dynamis* (see Meditation 2) can shift sick forms toward health.

Pondering 1

Are we born to be sick? to die? That would mean that our life had no sense, no mission or meaning.

Meditation 1

The meaning of our life cannot be put into words.

Foreword

In the gospels, we find reports about individual healings and indications about the general healing activity of the Lord. Matthew describes sixteen individual healings and five general examples of healing activity; in Mark the numbers are fifteen and three; in Luke seventeen and four; and while John has only four individual healings, they are very thoroughly described. Two examples of general healing activity are:

> For he had healed many insomuch that they had pressed upon him for to touch him, as many as had plagues... (Mark 3:10)

> And Jesus went about all Galilee, teaching in their synagogues, and preaching the gospel of the kingdom, and healing all manner of sickness and all manner of disease among the people. (Matthew 4:23)

The healings described in individualized accounts would today be considered psychosomatic phenomena:

they happen through the touch of the Lord, sometimes through merely the touch of his clothing and through his word, and sometimes only through his word. Very rarely is a material substance used, and then not as medicine but rather symbolically or as an aid to the patient's attention:

> When he had thus spoken, he spat on the ground, and made clay of the spittle, and he anointed the eyes of the blind man with the clay...(John 9:6) (See also Mark 8:23)

Therefore the first chapters here will describe the possibilities of psychosomatic healing and illness. Matthew, Mark and Luke each contain four accounts of individual healings that deal with the expulsion of unclean spirits; in John such healings are not mentioned.

Pondering 2

The healing power of the Lord is often characterized by the word *dynamis*:

> And it came to pass on a certain day, as he was teaching, and there were Pharisees and doctors of the law sitting by, which were come out of every town of Galilee, and Judea, and Jerusalem: and the power (*dynamis*) of the Lord was present to heal them. (Luke 5:17) (See also Luke 6:19, 8:46 and Mark 5:30)

This Greek word means capacity, power, ability, readiness, talent, validity, worth and meaning. For example, the "power" of a word or a sentence is its meaning. The verb *dynamai* means to be able to, to be capable of, to count as, to comprise, and to mean. We can try to think "power" and "meaning" as one.

Meditation 2

The power of the word is its meaning.

I.
PSYCHOSOMATICS

Anthropological Essentials

For a spiritual-scientific anthropology there are three ways in which the soul can influence the functions of the body:

- a) through the sentient body (soul-body), which is mediated by the vegetative nervous system;
- b) through the I-body (ego body) which also works on the body through the vegetative nervous system; and
- c) through the true I or Self, which is not inwardly connected to the body but operates on it as if from outside.

I.1. The Sentient Body

The sentient body is a mechanism through which the state of the soul can effect changes upon bodily functions without conscious intervention. For example, if the soul experiences itself as being in danger (whether truly or not), then a series of bodily functions are altered automatically:

the chemistry of the blood and of the brain, the blood-pressure and pulse, speed and depth of the breath, etc. We also find this phenomenon in animals, but for them the operation of the sentient body is tied to perception (the environment), while in human beings even fantasy can unleash the activity of the sentient body. In both cases (at least in higher animals) associative conditioning is possible. The sentient body always operates for the sake of biological health, to secure biological life in its proper functionality. In general, humans can neither consciously evoke nor prevent the biological changes involved. Even though mental states have an effect on the physical body through the sentient body (for instance, all the reactions of the vegetative nervous system), these phenomena are not considered "psychosomatic" today.

I.2. The I-Body

If you ask someone where he or she is, the answer will probably be "here," and that means where the body is. In other words, we experience ourselves as in the body and identical with it. This is not the situation near to the beginning of our time on earth, a fact which, for example, is evident when small children begin speaking of their "own" body in the third or even the second person. After a brief transition (nowadays at about 18 months), the child changes to the first person, and uses first person pronouns in the singular. This development marks a turning point in the child's life, and means that a certain point has been reached in the separation of consciousness from the child's prior feeling-participation in the human and non-human environment.

We can easily determine the point of separation when we pose the question of how the child learns the meanings of the audible and visible signs of language (words and gestures). No one explains anything to the child, nor can the child understand any explanation. The only solution to this riddle so far suggested by developmental psychology[1] is that the child, in its cognitive feeling, co-experiences the contents of the consciousnesses that surround it. This kind of participation grows weaker with age, and the turning point at about eighteen months (also the "memory point," since we generally remember back to this point in time) is the age after which cognitive feeling, the non-dualistic participation in the world, functions only weakly and occasionally.

The separation from participation in the world can be imagined as the development of a sheath or robe. This is not, of course, an image of something spatial, nor is it quite adequate, since the self-perception that arises ("proprioception" as it is known in psychology) extends to the inner part of the body if something there is not functioning healthily (for example, in pain). This "self-perception" or "experience of the body" is notably non-cognitive: we don't perceive the body anatomically; rather, we perceive only a more or less localizable sensation. For example, in the case of a headache, we experience pain in our skull but it tells us nothing about what is going on in the brain. In the same way, we feel pain or itching when we cough, without learning anything about the lungs or the bronchial tubes.

This sheath is also related to egotism; the feeling of "me" is egotism's first seed. We perceive this me-feeling, and so it forms the beginning of self-awareness. It seems at first glance to be self-awareness on the part of the observer; instead it is actually one's awareness misattributed to the sensation being observed—as if someone confused himself with his own image in a mirror (a comparison used by many authors).

The me-feeling and its associated self-awareness form the basis of what is generally called the *lower human being* or the habitual human or the memory-human, in the sense of the notion that the I or self consists merely in the totality of one's experiences, memories, habits and learning. We can call this total formation the "I-body."[2] It consists of fixed forms. We tend to "forget" that experiences, memories and so on presuppose a subject *whose* experiences, memories and so forth they are.

The I-body can operate psychosomatically, mostly in a negative sense, causing disturbances and even diseases. This shows up in our passions and dependencies (alcohol, drugs, etc.), where it works without any concern for biological health, mostly even working against it.

The development of the me-feeling is known, in many of the world's spiritual traditions, as the Fall of Man.

Pondering 3

What is the difference between the sentient body and the I-body? How do we experience them?

Meditation 3

Our normal sense of self is like a mirror image—but whose?

I.3. *The Spiritual Essence of the Human Being*

Acording to the recent observations of child psychologists, children are individuals from the very start. Their individuality is shown by their very selective imitation, and by their various responses to influences from without, as in the phenomenon of "resilience." Along with inheritance and environmental influence, individuality is the third factor that directs our life.

To clarify the concept of "spiritual essence," we can turn to the concept "meaning." A word, for example, consists of its sign-side (which may be acoustic or visual; the sense-perceptible aspect of the word), and also of its meaning-side. The latter cannot be perceived by the senses. If we pose the question as to what a meaning is "made of," what it consists in, then it is easy to see that it is not made of anything material (neither solid, liquid, gaseous, nor from elementary particles, etc.); instead, it is a spiritual form. Such forms are, on the one hand, non-material, and on the other hand they *are* meaningful, or rather they are meanings, and can be understood (the sign, the sense-perceptible part, is never understood). As long as we human beings are able to understand meanings, we have access to a meaning-potential similar to the meanings themselves; but the meanings as they come to us are already formed, whereas the capacity to understand them is itself form-free. This form-free capacity can then be fit, or poured, into every form of meaning. What isn't material can neither be perceived nor understood through materiality. Humans make and understand meanings through their spiritual essence.

The spiritual essence of the human being appears in the *superconscious* functions of consciousness and in the communicative functions of the body. For example, the *process* of thinking is superconscious; that is, we don't know how we think—in contrast to the knowledge of, for example, how we clean our shoes. We also do not experience the "how" of many biological processes but, of course, our most conscious soul-function, thinking, doesn't originate in them. Similarly, we know little of how we perceive: that is, we don't experience the process of how the perception comes about, but only the result of the process, the percept, the already-perceived.

When we say that we don't experience these processes, we are not speaking of their physiological, nervous, chemical and other bases. For these bases are all consequences of the processes within consciousness; they are secondary phenomena, even if they might not be secondary in a temporal sense. For example: let us assume that we can determine what takes place in the brain, or elsewhere in the body, when we have understood something. This determination could only take place because of the normal experience in consciousness that "I understand." And if, in the brain, a little green lamp went on when we thought or said something, we could only know what the signal meant through recourse to conscious awareness. Only our own awareness of it can "tell" us what is happening at the same time as the lighting of the little lamp.

Awareness originates in the superconscious. But since our superconsciousness is not conscious, we normally do not experience our capacities themselves, but only their products. The central capacity of the human being is attention, which is also not experienced in itself but only in its objects. Superconsciousness also applies to the bodily communicative capacities, whose prototype is speech. We don't know how we speak. We don't know the compli-cated movements of our own speech organs. We only know the meaning of what we say once it has already appeared in language, even though it must have already been there superconsciously for us to be able to choose the language, the words and the grammatical forms—and this "choice" also takes place superconsciously.

Though the capacities are surely more *real* (more effective) than their products, still we don't experience them. In comparison with their products they are *form-free*, and just this makes new products possible. The capacity to write poetry is the source of poems, and so it is logically more "real" than they are, even if it is never experienced in itself.

Pondering 4

How do we know about the superconscious? What is "reality" if we don't experience the part of our being that creates all effects—our capacities?

Meditation 4

We experience the given, conscious "reality" through superconscious capacities. But is this *experience* at all?

I.4. The Link between the Spiritual Being and the Inherited Body

It follows from the very nature of the problem that we know little about the connection between the two parts of the human being, especially at the beginning of life. However, intuitive (meditative) research reveals some-thing about the connection of the two parts, and such research can be confirmed to a further extent through external observation. In this way we can distinguish fairly well between two phases in the life of the small child: the time before and the time following the development of proprioception.

Before this turning point (which also involves the appearance of first person pronouns), the body is almost like any other thing for the spiritual being who speaks through it (and feels and wills). This is why that spiritual being, the small child, speaks about the body in the third person. The speaking being is a spiritual being. It uses the body to speak and to perceive, but does not feel itself to be identical with it. When "self-perception" arises (and by "self" here we mean the sensation of the body) it causes various changes in the life of consciousness.

Above all, a kind of self-consciousness comes about that reveals itself in the use of pronouns as described above. There are other signs in language, for example the use of *connection-words* (such as *how, perhaps, certainly*), words that appear after the turning point, and none of which are pictorial or sense-perceptible.

The control of non-communicative bodily movements begins. Communicative movements (such as eye-contact, smiling, laughing, speaking, body-language) can already be observed before the turning point. Intentional movements of the limbs presuppose the (non-anatomical) sensation of these limbs. The body's situation from moment to moment is perceived; bumping against objects in space comes to an end.

A localized sense of pain develops, enabling the child to show what part of the body hurts. As is well known, this is impossible beforehand: the child seems to experience every pain in its belly.

The body's senses begin to be used, either for the first time or more consciously. Concomitant with the afore-mentioned sense of movement, the sense of touch, the sense of warmth, and the sense of balance come more and more into play. The connection of these senses with the separating "robe" becomes clear from those cases where the activity of these senses is weak or absent (autism, certain types of dyslexia, and other deviations from so-called "normal development").

As a result of this change in the relationship of the spiritual being to the body, with the exception of more or less brief periods of functioning, cognitive feeling (as referred to above) weakens and even ceases. By contrast, the self-sensing of the body increases and extends to the realm of the soul where it is familiar as egotism. This is the kernel of the I-body and so of most negative emotions (non-cognitive forms of feeling), such as anger, envy, jealousy, etc., but it is also the source of conflicts (which are always emotionally laden, otherwise we do not term them conflicts).

In general we can say that through the development of proprioception, the non-dualistic participation in the world comes to an end and so does the "communal consciousness" that enables the child cognitively to feel the meanings of words and grammatical forms immediately and without signs.

Pondering 5

What is the difference between communicative and non-communicative use of the body? Where is the attention during communicative use of the body?

I.5. Changes in Attentiveness

Apart from the activity of the sentient body (the vegetative nervous system), the soul-spiritual life of the child is taken up with immersion in the world. By "world" we mean what is sense-perceptible, the soul-world of the human environment, and also the spiritual world as the source of intuitions among adults and also the common source of superconscious abilities of human beings, for example, the commonality of thinking. Although the different languages shape the child's thinking differently, translation from one language to another (despite its limitations) is possible, and in Western civilization thinking emancipates itself early on from the mother tongue, and in fact from all language.

The capacity for devotion, absorption, and immersion is a heightened attentiveness. In adults, such absorption is generally limited to special circumstances such as artistic/aesthetic appreciation, particular interest for a theme, or work activities. In all these cases, absorption is accompanied by self-forgetting, that is, during absorption the me-feeling (or simply the me) is extinguished. In the small child this is the predominant state, since self-feeling only comes about gradually. In adults, everyday attention oscillates very quickly between its objects and the sense of "me."

If we observe the ongoing stream of attention in an adult, which is not very difficult to do, then we can distinguish two components. One component, normally very briefly, perceives each object. The absorption is momentary and includes a self-forgetting that, because of its brevity, is not experienced consciously. Still, we can say that in every perception of an object (including inwardly perceived objects), attention becomes identical

with what it perceives, as a spectator in the theater identifies with the action on stage, or as my thinking has to
slip into the form of the other person's thought—that is,
identify with it—if I am to understand it.

This capacity to identify, then, is one component of
attention. At the same time, in every experience, and
without thinking about it, we know implicitly that it is
our experience, that "I" (whatever I may mean by this)
am the subject of the experience. The component of
attention that helps us to reach this knowledge could be
called the *witnessing* component. We might imagine that
this part of attention does not become the object, that
it does not go through the metamorphosis. For, at first,
the witness seems to be identical with the me (-feeling).
Yet, in the experience of deep self-forgetting the implicit
witness is still present; otherwise, on returning from self-
forgetting we could not report what was experienced
during the self-forgetting. And, in fact, we can report on
it all the more exactly the deeper the self-forgetting was.
This demonstrates that the witness is not identical with
either the "me" or the everyday "I."

In the small child, these two components are
completely un-separated before the turning point. In
other words, the world is not "experienced" dualistically, where there is a relationship between a subject
and an object. Rather, there is a kind of one-ness with
the world, so that we can even wonder whether it is an
"experience" at all. In any case, we generally do not
remember this part of our lives, where the witnessing
component of attention is not separated from the other
and so is not actually a witness.

Through their earlier self-awareness, the new generation of children[3] differs from what has been thus far

described here. They differ even before encountering the turning point, and they therefore differ also in their ability to remember earlier events.

The separation of the two components of attention evidently occurs during the turning point; this is also why it becomes the first foothold of memory. From that point on, a witness is present. The cognitive/feeling component becomes sharply reduced, because it changes largely into a me-feeling (*autoperception*), becoming a form (the I-body) and so sacrificing its form-freedom, its capacity to cognize or pour itself into all objects. The separating robe consists at first of the earlier self-feeling/identifying component. Later, thinking and willing aspects are woven into habitual forms as well, and the whole comprises what psychology knows as the subconscious. This consists in tough, hard-to-dissolve forms,[4] while the superconscious, the capacity-human, represents form-free attentiveness—for instance thinking, seeing, hearing and other kinds of attention. The subconscious habit-formation belongs to the I-body. It is considered the source of possible psychosomatic illnesses.

The separation of the two streams of attention has a dual face. First, it secures the preliminary independence of the human being. It seals us off from the world and gives rise to the initial, mostly egotistical self-awareness. Second, it can become destructive both for the person in question and also for the world; this is so because the separation threatens real understanding of both human beings and of the world.

If the separation is inadequate, however, there is a different kind of dual effect. Its positive side can be called openness (see Foreword, above), and that means capacities—openness for intuitions, insights. At the same time though, "open" people today—those who are less separated than the average—encounter numerous difficulties. They can respond to intellectual challenges only with much effort or insufficiently, and they are exposed, by the lack of a thick, protective robe, to mental and psychiatric disease. The latter symptoms are generally compensatory efforts against their being unprotected and over-sensitive.

Meditation 5

I forget myself in absorption.

I.6. The True I or Self

The spiritual being of the human manifests in life as the superconscious capacity of attention, the inner light. Without special training, we do not experience attention as such, that is to say, form-free, objectless, "empty." If, through a training in consciousness, it becomes experiential, then the true Self, the true I, which lay as if asleep within the stream of our attentiveness, awakes. Because of its presence, even when it is not self-aware, we know that every experience is *our* experience.

When it awakes, the spiritual being becomes aware of itself, which is not like becoming aware of an object as occurs in the being's normal functioning. This awareness-of-self experience is possible in a variety of qualities: various kinds of attention become self-aware—the attention of thinking/mental-picturing, the attention in feeling-knowing, the attention in willing-knowing, etc. This true self-experience was and is the primary goal of every spiritual tradition. Today it can be called the I AM experience;

in the New Testament, the person who experiences it is called a "son of the light."[5] In Zen Buddhism, the identical experience is referred to as "seeing your Buddha nature," or "seeing your own nature" (that is, the attention).[6] In every tradition, and today as well, the schooling of consciousness consists in the limitless intensification of attention, beginning always with the most conscious and autonomous kind of attention—today, in the West, it is the attention of thinking and mental-picturing.

We already mentioned that the true Self can (positively) affect the body, since it is independent of the body in its self-experience.

What we call our "I" in everyday consciousness can be considered a mirror image (generally distorted) of the true I. In the healings in the New Testament, this true Self of the sick person, or that of his or her representative, has to either flash forth or at least be touched upon.

Summary and Supplement

1) Our separation from the world happens in consciousness. Everything else—such as the body—is simply given. This is why the effect of the robe was described in terms of changes in consciousness. Even the robe itself consists in formed feeling-attention, or self-feeling-attention.

2) The separation is by no means absolute. In every experience consciousness emerges for a moment from out of separation, though this process is so brief that it is not noticed.

3) Since the true I, the element that experiences reality, is not conscious, since its existence is generally not even

34

guessed at, experience is mis-attributed to its mirror image, which is the everyday I, the habitual human.

4) The separating sheath or robe makes possible the first, preliminary self-awareness, without which no further development, no freedom, therefore no human creativity, would be possible. But neither could what religions call evil have any place in us; that is the price of freedom. Without this sheath, the human being would simply be a continuation of the (spiritual) world.

5) All specifically human capacities are, as such, super-conscious, in other words ontologically "given." These capacities—not developed or invented by human beings—are vestiges of a purely spiritual existence from out of which the spiritual being descends to "earth," to a connection with the body.

Meditation 6

(Epistle of James 1:17) Every good gift and every perfect gift is from above, and cometh down from the Father of lights, with whom is no variableness, neither shadow of turning.

II.

THE ANTHROPOLOGICAL BASIS OF HEALING IN THE LANGUAGE OF THE NEW TESTAMENT

II.1. *The One from Above*

According to an old Orphic text, the human being is a "child of Earth and of the starry Heavens." This saying points to the polar nature of the human being, in which the "earthly" means not only the physical body, but above all the "earthly" awareness, just as the stars in heaven do not refer to the visible heavenly bodies, but to the spiritual star of the human being (see Chapter V.2). In the New Testament, this polarity appears in the expressions "from above" and "from below," "born from above," "coming from above," and also through the contrast between "spirit" and "flesh."

As a starting point to understanding the polarity more exactly, we can take the third chapter of the Gospel of John. The Lord says to Nicodemus (John 3:3), "Verily, verily I say unto thee: except a man be born from above, he cannot see the kingdom of God." Luther and most other translators write "again" for the Greek word *anothen* ("from above"). The word has both meanings, but here it is used in the sense of "down from above."

Zwingli translates the word correctly, as "from above," and notes in a footnote, "The word also means 'again'; that is why Nicodemus could misunderstand it." Compare John 3:4: "Nicodemus saith unto him: How can a man be born when he is old? Can he enter a second time into his mother's womb and be born?" In John 19:11 the sense of the word is unambiguously "from above" (compare Kühlewind, *The Kingdom of God*, "What doesn't belong to the Kingdom").

Verse 7 repeats, "Marvel not that I said unto thee, Ye must be born from above." In the same chapter John the Baptist says: "He that cometh from above is above all: he that is of the earth is earthly, and speaketh of the earth: he that cometh from heaven is above all" (John 3:31).

Behind the sentences cited above, there is a meditative content that cannot be communicated as information, toward which we can only hint. The one "from above" is evidently an individual who has realized the I AM experience at the highest level. This is also the meaning of the words in John 8:23: "Ye are from beneath; I am from above: ye are of this world; I am not of this world."

At the end of the story the Lord says to Pilate, "My kingdom is not of this world" (John 18:36). The one from above can heal diseases of the body or of the soul and the spirit, because his Self is "above all," *independent* of all. In John 3:6 we read, "That which is born of the flesh is flesh; and that which is born of the Spirit is spirit." The meaning of the word "flesh" in this instance (see Kühlewind, *The Renewal of the Holy Spirit*, "The Flesh") obviously is not "muscles," but refers instead to the weak part of the soul that clings to the flesh. The same meaning is apparent in sentences like "The spirit is willing but the fles is weak" (Matthew 26:41; Mark 14:38), or "to walk after the flesh" (Romans 8:1), or the passage in Galatians 5:17-20:

> For the flesh lusteth against the Spirit, and the Spirit against the flesh: and these are contrary the one to the other: so that ye cannot do the things that ye would.... Now the works of the flesh are manifest, which are these: Adultery, fornication, uncleanness....

There follows a long catalogue of the sins that derive from the "flesh." What is "born" either from the flesh or the spirit are the impulses, thoughts, and mental pictures within us that determine our lives.

Every human being is "born" from above and from below, and the link between these two elements determines our life, our diseases, and our death. In the environment of the Lord, this changing, changeable connection and its determination of a person's life seems to have been more or less conscious, while in the last centuries awareness of it has disappeared almost entirely. However, in the last few decades, this awareness has re-emerged increasingly in the form of psychosomatic effects. Of course this phenomenon comes to light in an incomplete fashion since our culture, and academically recognized science, refuses to recognize the "spiritual" almost entirely, and acknowledges the "soul" almost exclusively as an epiphenomenon— though our culture has been allowing more and more significance to it.

Pondering 6

Where do we notice "the one from above"?

Meditation 7

We grow from above.

Meditation 8

The one coming from above is above all.

II.2 *Spiritual Healing*

Spiritual healing means that the "one from above" heals the lower part of us, which is the only part of us that can become sick. It may be a sickness of the body or of the soul (e.g., possession by demons). For healing, the higher being has to be made independent of the lower. The part of the higher being that has connected itself to the "robe" has to be freed from this connection so that the higher self can act on it as if from outside. Even in everyday life we can forget "ourselves," our me-feeling, to a certain extent, as for example in artistic, creative activity or in prayer. To be healed we need a deep, total "self-forgetting," so that we are present only in the heights.

These spiritual healings were not rare in earlier phases of the evolution of consciousness, and are still possible today in many "non-civilized" regions wherever the *me* is undeveloped. In these cases, the everyday consciousness was and is extinguished through various procedures, similar or identical to the earlier initiation rites that operated through a dislocation of one's awareness. We can describe these processes as very deep examples of self-forgetting. This is how John the Baptist worked, holding the person to be baptized under water to the brink of death (which is why he needed "much water," cf. John 3:23).[7]

The new Christian baptism (with "fire and the holy spirit"), is a purely inward way, accomplished without the extinction of consciousness, though it does involve a radical transformation of it. Today, a schooling of consciousness begins in everyday awareness and leads continually, without loss of consciousness, to the "forgetting" of the *me*. This new kind of initiation goes along with a new potential for healing: in the healings of the New Testament, the healed person is perfectly awake, consciousness is neither asleep nor extinguished. At first the Lord is present at the healings; later the disciples heal and, after Golgotha, the apostles as well.

II.3. Preconditions for Spiritual Healing

Death and disease of the body have their origin in the Fall. Today, this is what makes the I-body develop. For spiritual healing to come about, the pre-Fall state has to be re-instated, at least for an instant. This is equivalent to the dissolution of the I-body or freedom from sins (forgiveness of sins), which is also called "faith" in the New Testament: a complete certainty, surety without the slightest shadow of doubt—the experienced connection with the true Self or I. It is possible for the whole of someone's attention to be concentrated in the true I through the presence of the Lord or His representative, through the inductive effect of His (or their) openness. Openness tends to open other people, though this effect can be warded off, leading to hatred toward the one who is open.

The separating robe makes the body accessible to earthly consciousness, which is based on proprioception; at the same time, the body becomes inaccessible to higher, spiritual superconsciousness, apart from its use in communicative abilities.[8] This is why, for spiritual healing to take place, the separation has to be lifted. There are two expressions for this lifting in the Gospels: faith, and being freed from one's sins.

Faith

When consciousness is linked to its superconscious source, the person experiences doubt-free certainty. The word for faith in Greek is pistis, and it means above all security and surety. So the meaning of "faith" in the New Testament is certainty. Certainty can only be complete certainty—a lesser certainty can not be called certainty at all.

The attentiveness of the small child is still unified. It is a feeling that has not yet been led through the channels of the senses or thinking, that has not yet been broken up. For adults, attention is either the attention of seeing or hearing or tasting, etc. Unbroken, entire attention is faith.

Where there is a concept and even a word for this certainty, the content of the concept is also conscious—which means that the content is no longer given, and also that its opposite, in this case the lack of belief, is known about and conscious. So pistis means a state of the soul in which it has certainty and also knows about having the certainty. In other words: there is a witness there, and so it (the certainty) can be called an experience. If the connection between consciousness and its source is a naturally given thing, we cannot speak of it, it is not an experience, and there is no witness present; it is a participatory existence, an identity. At the beginning of the twentieth century this kind of existence was called "participatory consciousness" by ethnologists when they encountered it in archaic cultures.

Faith is an experienced certainty: connection with the spirit, which is not necessarily given. It is in no way a weaker substitute for knowledge ("I believe it because I can't know it"), but rather a knowledge, feeling, surety, whose conviction is unarguable—the certainty of one's own roots in divinity. Faith is like an intuition, that is, an experience, but in healing it has *duration*, whether for a fraction of a second or for a half an hour. Duration means that it is not just a flash.

Faith replaces, as an experience, the earlier spiritual perception of pre-Christian religiosity, the perception of spiritual beings and the meaning of the created world, which was also direct experience. This change is particularly emphasized by St. Paul when he writes, for example in 2 Corinthians 5:6-7: "...whilst we are at home in the body, we are absent from the Lord: (for we walk by faith, not by sight)." Not in seeing, or (since the Greek word *eidos* also means image, appearance) "not in the appearance of eternal glory" as the Zwingli translation adds. Paul speaks in a similar way in the famous passage of 1 Corinthians 13:12,13: "For now we see through a glass, darkly; but then face to face: now I know in part; but then I shall know even as also I am known. And now abideth faith, hope, charity...." The piecework of cognition will one day be subsumed within a non-dualistic way of knowing. Until then, there remain to us faith, hope, and love as means of cognition.

Faith is not seeing: "No man hath seen God..." (John 1:18), but the non-imagistic feeling of certainty which replaces the immediate image-experience of divinity; it is faith that became, at the beginning of Christianity, the new form of connection to the Source. It is not a belief "in" anything; it is the actually un-nameable absolute certainty of being in a meaningful world.

The first letter by Timothy refers to the "mystery of faith in a pure conscience" (1 Timothy 3:9). In the first letter by Peter we can find out in what this mystery consists: "...the goal of your faith [is] the blessedness of souls"—as Zwingli puts it. But the word *telos* (here translated as "goal") means *completion, performance, fulfillment, exit, result, highpoint, initiation*. And soteria ("blessedness") is used for *sustenance, saving, redemption, certainty, security*. "The mystery of faith in a pure conscience" therefore attains a much deeper significance. Conscience and faith are linked in the letter to Hebrews (10:22):

> Let us draw near with a true heart in full assurance of faith, having our hearts sprinkled from an evil conscience, and our bodies washed with pure water...

and in the first letter of Timothy (1:5; 3:9)—with an impure conscience no faith—that is to say, no certainty—is possible.

If conscience is pure, there is no barrier between everyday consciousness and its superconscious sources. This does not yet mean that a connection is established, i.e., that faith becomes experience. Experience is the marker or sign of an effective connection upward, which can lead to healing. Certainty can blaze forth, but for healing to occur it must have duration. All of the healing stories testify to this. Today it is possible once again to approach the experience of spirituality through a schooling of consciousness. This has to do with the development of consciousness that has taken place through Christianity in the last 2,000 years.

Pondering 7

Why is our certainty never complete? What would be the condition for its being so?

Sins and Their Forgiveness

We can have no clear ("pure") conscience if we feel sinful—and who does not? It is helpful to know what the words "sinful," "sin," "error" have as meanings and connotations in other languages, so as better and more variously to feel our way into them. They are, after all, used frequently in regard to the healings in the New Testament.

The verb *hamartano*, normally translated as "to sin," means originally "to miss the goal or target"; secondary meanings are "not to achieve, to err, to lose, to give up, to go astray, to sin, to withhold." It is remarkable, and well worth a meditation, that in Greek and also in Hebrew (the word *chet*) the word for "sin" means to miss one's goal or target. In this difference from us, a very different worldview is encoded. It is the same with the noun "*hamartema*," which means primarily "mistake, error." The word normally translated as "mistake," *paraptoma*, is used for "oversight, mistake, loss"; the corresponding verb *parapito* means primarily "to fall to one side, to stumble on something accidentally, to arrive somewhere, to run or hurry alongside"; and secondarily, "to err, mistake." According to the implicit worldview here, the Good, the True, and hitting one's mark is the more original deed, and sin is a deviation from this originary gift.

The "forgiveness of sins"—a phrase that recurs often in regard to the healings—means to be freed from error; it means the possibility of return to the right path, in the sense of one's calling. What is translated as "forgive, forgiveness," comes from the verb *aphiemi*, means primarily "to send away, send off, leave free, let go, give away, let sound forth, throw away, give up, leave undone." In the Our Father, this verb is used (Matthew 6:12, Luke 11:4) as in "let our sins go." And this word also often appears in accounts of the healings.

Even in the opening moments of Christianity, the forgiveness of sins was mentioned. The Baptist preaches about "baptism of change of sense for the remission (forgiveness) of sins." What I call "change of sense" is normally translated as "repentance," though the Greek term for it, *metanoia*, is literally "change of direction in the *nous* or 'sense'." This conjunction of terms is also to be found in Luke 3:3 ("And he came into all the country about Jordan, preaching the baptism of repentance for the remission of sins...") as well as in the Acts 2:38, 5:31, 13;38, 26:18. Instead of "forgiveness," it would be more accurate to speak of a "lifting" of sin or "liberation" from sin.

The corresponding noun *aphesis* means "sending forth, expedition (of carts), unloading, separation, remit, divorce, release (e.g., of prisoners), freeing."

The change of "sense" can go so far that a person is released, at least for a time, from the lower self—which alone can be sinful. This is what the Baptist means by "change of sense unto (*eis* = "into") freedom from sins." This freeing is the release of the separating robe and from the related habits, dependencies, passions, egotism, from the "flesh" as the source of sins:

> For the flesh lusteth against the Spirit, and the Spirit against the flesh: and these are contrary the one to the other: so that ye cannot do the things that ye would. But if ye be led of the Spirit, ye are not under the law. Now the works of the flesh are manifest, which are these: Adultery, fornication, uncleanness, lasciviousness, idolatry, witchcraft, hatred, variance, emulations, wrath, strife, seditions, heresies, envyings, murders, drunkenness, revellings, and such like: of the which I tell you before, as I have also told you in time past, that they which do such things shall not inherit the kingdom of God. (Gal 5:17-20)

Through freedom from sins, *faith*, or all-encompassing certainty, is produced that connection to what is above, which is necessary for healing.

Pondering 8

What is the difference between "missing the mark" and "sinning"?

Meditation 9

You are freed from your sins.

II.4. The Unity of the Healings

From the preceding chapters we can see that in the absence of the separating robe, or if it were not to develop at all, human beings would live in a consciousness common to all. This is evident in small children, as well as in archaic peoples who, as reports indicate, can communicate among themselves at a distance without signs. In the Bible the cessation of this ability is portrayed in the story of the Tower of Babel. Silent, signless communication, directed by the attention—ceases, and there remains only the languages of the different peoples, which were already present (Genesis, Chapter 10), but through which the various peoples could not understand one another.

The original signless (or "direct") communication is even active today, behind our words and signs. Words can never be unambiguous. (This is so apart from technical/scientific terms, which in turn must be defined by undefinable words from earlier languages.) What allows for mutual understanding is "good will," or "feeling connected," or "you already know what I mean"—in short, the realm of intuitive, common meaning in which the higher self always lives.

Through the temporary dissolution of what separates us, which is called "freedom from sins" or "faith," the sick person, or a representative, gets lifted into the realm of signless understanding, where the Healer is also present. The primary state, still untouched by errors, is reproduced for a time. People then live in their higher being, independent of the lower being, and are therefore capable, with the Lord's help, to have a healing effect on this lower being.

By "self-forgetting" the person rises to the true Self, and from there, through the Lord, to the Beginning—the state of the world in which no form is yet present. This state is the "place"—ever-present, ever to be sought—that is called *arche*, the realm of primal beginning, before the Fall, before any forms arose but from which they arise.

In the spiritual, world being *is* communicating; there, human spiritual beings work together in steady communication. It is clear that this primal communication is related to healing.

In *arche*, one I-being lives with another immediately, without mediation, with nothing in between them, light within light. *That* is the real healing *touch*, whose symbol or suggestive image is outer touch in the New Testament.

To a limited, partial extent the higher being has an effect on all the communicative activities of the body, above all in speaking. The movement of the speech-organs, the emergence of speech-intention (still super-linguistic), the finding of the corresponding words and the manner of expression—all these are superconscious, i.e., the being or the activity of the higher self. If the relationship of the spiritual being to the whole of the body were like its relationship to the organs of speech during speaking, then a person would speak with the whole of his or her body, and makes signs with it—an independent art of movement. If the activity of the spiritual being extended to the functionality of the limbs, the form, the state of the body, then we would be in a position to heal—just as the healing of wounds now goes on independently of everyday consciousness. This is what seems to be happening in the bodily healings in the New Testament. For healings at a distance (Matthew 8:6; 15:22; Mark 7:25; Luke 7:1; John 4:46) we have to find still other concepts, as we do for the "psychiatric" healing of the possessed.

III.

The "Psychiatric" Healings

The healings of the possessed take place through the Word of the Lord: the sick people are not touched, nor do they touch the Lord (before being healed). They are possessed by demons or by unclean spirits, sometimes by dumb or evil spirits as well. The word "devil," as Luther used in his translations, actually does not appear in the exorcism stories of the New Testament; Zwingli is more exact in his version of the text. So we will first characterize the unclean spirits, or demons, just as they are described, and then the way in which the Lord heals those who are possessed.

III.1. The Description of Demons

The expressions "demon" and "unclean spirit" are used synonymously in the synoptic Gospels; *daemon-izzomenoi*, or "possessed," is only in Matthew and Mark; while none of these words, or any healing of the soul, is mentioned in the John Gospel. The demons, or those possessed by them, are portrayed with certain characteristics and ways of behavior. The story of the two possessed men (Matthew 8:28-32) is typical:

> And when he was come to the other side into the country of the Gergesenes, there met him two possesssed with demons, coming out of the tombs, exceeding fierce, so that no man might pass by that way. And behold, they cried out, saying, What have we to do with thee, Jesus, thou Son of God? art thou come hither to torment us before the time? And there was a good way off from them a herd of many swine feeding. So the demons besought him, saying: If thou cast us out, suffer us to go away into the herd of swine. And he said unto them, Go. And when they were come out, they went into the herd of swine; and, behold, the whole herd of swine ran violently down a steep place into the sea, and perished in the waters.

The same healing is given again with slight changes in Mark (1:7) and in Luke (8:26). According to Mark:

> And when he was come out of the ship, immediately there met him out of the tombs a man with an unclean spirit. Who had his dwelling among the tombs, and no man could bind him, no, not with chains: Because that he had been often bound with fetters and chains, and the chains had been plucked asunder by him, and the fetters broken in pieces: neither could any man tame him. And always, night and day, he was in the mountains, and in the tombs, crying and cutting himself with

stones. But when he saw Jesus afar off, he ran and worshipped him. And cried with a loud voice, and said, what have I to do with thee, Jesus, thou Son of the most high God? I adjure thee by god, that thou torment me not. For he said unto him, come out of the man, thou unclean spirit. And he asked him, What is thy name? And he answered, saying, My name is Legion: for we are many.

What follows corresponds to the version in Matthew. The most characteristic features of the demons are these:

1) The person possessed has unusual physical strength;
2) The demons recognize the Lord;
3) They speak in the plural, even if there is only one person possessed;
4) in many stories, they tear at the possessed person and throw him or her to the ground, especially during the healing.

1) Physical strength is well known in raging psychotic patients. It comes from the constellation of bodily members in which the I, the higher Self, moves the lower, bodily self as if from outside.[9]

2) Recognition of the Lord, like the ability to perceive the essence behind the appearance, is not given to "healthy" people. Yet it is characteristic for many handicapped people, autists, and in general for small children—and today for the "difficult" children of the new generation. It is linked with the momentary release from proprioception, from the separating robe.

3) Demons are never present in the possessed person one at a time, as we see in both Mark 1:23 and Luke 4:33.

> And there was in their synagogue a man with an unclean spirit; and he cried out, saying, Let us alone: what have we to do with thee, thou Jesus of Nazareth? Art thou come to destroy us? I know thee who thou art, the Holy One of God.

Their plural nature corresponds to the modern experience that there is always a plurality of forms in the subconscious, which are "senseless" or "meaningless"—that is, non-communicative.[10]

4) Those who are mentally ill often experience bodily movements that are not led by their conscious will, as also in cases of cramp or in epileptic fits. These gestures can also be mixed, as in the stories of those possessed (Luke 8.28):

> When he saw Jesus, he cried out, and fell down before him, and with a loud voice said What have I to do with thee, Jesus, thou Son of God most high? I beseech thee, torment me not. (Luke 8:28) (See also Matthew 8:28; Mark 5:7.)

The possessed person throws himself at Jesus' feet as if to ask for help, but it is the demon who then speaks through his words.

In several Gospel accounts we read that the Lord forbids the demons to reveal him.

And he healed many that were sick of diverse
diseases, and cast out many devils; and suffered
not the devils to speak, because they knew him.
(Mark 1:34) (See also Mark 3:11, Luke 4:41.)

Meditation 10

The demons are always many.

III.2. What are the Demons?

Among archaic peoples, demons were (and are) familiar as negative spiritual beings alongside good spirits
(angels). Modern peoples no longer have the experiences
described in the New Testament, but we can very well
notice independent "forces," processes, and impulses
in our own souls. These may arise in our consciousness without, or even against, our conscious will, and
mislead us into actions that, if we think them through
clearly, we do not intend doing, but against which we
are incapable of marshalling sufficient resistance. Such
independent elements in the soul reveal themselves at
various levels, with various potencies. In any exercise of
concentration,[11] such as concentrating on a man-made
object, we can almost always experience distractions
(associations); they are the mildest, weakest independent
elements, though they can be very disruptive to the exercise. More serious are obsessive thoughts and compulsions, which we today recognize as pathological; lesser
compulsions are common and often unconscious. In our
time, independent elements such as these are included
within the everyday sense of self, and are generally considered part of the personality. That is, although equipped
with a certain independence, they are at least perceived,

even temporally tolerated, often also fought against. The situation is more difficult when the everyday self identifies with one or more independent elements, and can no longer distinguish between them and its own nature.

In earlier times when the everyday I (which consists in free forces of attention outside the I-body) was far less strongly developed, the separate, unconscious forms[12] were much more independent of the human center, for this center was weaker, less self-aware, and allowed itself to be determined more by forces from above and below, feeling itself compelled by these forces. This kind of experience was very clearly described by St. Paul. We read, for example, in Romans 7:15-20:

> For that which I do I understand not: for what I would, that do I not; but what I hate, that do I. If then I do that which I would not, I consent unto the law that it is good. Now then it is no more I that do it, but sin that dwelleth in me. For I know that in me (that is, in my flesh) dwelleth no good thing: for to will is present with me; but how to perform that which is good I find not. For the good that I would I do not: but the evil which I would not, that I do. Now if I do that I would not, it is no more I that do it, but sin that dwelleth in me.

We have an insight here into what is called sin, since it has such independence that it arises against human will; and it lives in the "flesh." So the "forgiveness of sins" acquires a special meaning: it is equivalent to the momentary purging of these independent elements. Neither the good nor the evil independent elements are ascribed to the human center: instead, either God or sin affects the soul.

> For it is God that worketh in you both to will and
> to do for the sake of *eudokia*. (Philippians 2:13,
> c.f. 2 Cor 3:5)[13]

At least since Freud, we know that unconscious forms seem equipped with a certain "intelligence" that helps them prevail. This trait gives them a kind of being, as if they were conscious or at least instinctive entities—even with a goal-directed slyness about them.

If we go back still further in time, into the course of the evolution of consciousness, we find ever-diminishing self-awareness in everyday consciousness, since the separating robe is ever less powerful. If, in these earlier periods, an independent formation arises within the soul, it differs from our current experience in two ways. On the one hand, the formation can be large—even limitless (that is, it can for a time completely control the person in question); on the other hand, what we know today as its "intelligence" or capacity to prevail can emerge as expressed, open resistance to every attempt at improvement or healing. This brings us to the demons of the New Testament. In various spiritual traditions, independent formations within the soul are known as "elementary beings," and definitely considered as equipped with intelligence and will. In the New Testament, they show this by recognizing the Lord as God's son (Matthew 3:11, 8:32; Luke 4:41). They can also name him by his name, as "Jesus of Nazareth, the holy one of God" (Mark 1:23), "son of the highest God" (Mark 5:7; Luke 8:28), and they know about his power to drive them out of those they possess. This goes beyond the "slyness" of the subconscious and has to be considered further.

The "zoology" of the demons shows general traits that cannot be found in the perceptual world, and even contradict it. One was already mentioned: that the demons always arise in the plural, as many. More exactly: like elementary beings, they cannot be counted; their number changes continually according to influences, even through the act of counting them. There is an indistinctness here, as in particle physics. The other trait: to be sure, the demons arose from the possessed person's forces of attention, yet nothing is missing from the person's attentiveness after the expulsion—as love, for example, does not diminish by being given away.

III.3. The Expulsion of Demons through the Word of the Lord

All healings involving the expulsion of demons take place through the Word. This is emphasized explicitly in some accounts (Mark 8:16), but simply described in most of them. The Lord rebukes ("threatens" in Luther and Zwingli) the unclean spirits, or commands them to leave the person.

The Greek word for "threaten" or "rebuke," *epitimao*, has many meanings; those that apply here are "reproach, scold, rebuke." *Timao* means "esteem, honor, observe, consider" (apart from many derived meanings).

Let us consider two typical healings: the possessed man in the synagogue (Mark 1:23, Luke 4:35) and the story we have already looked at (involving two people according to Matthew 8:32, one according to Mark 5:7 and Luke 8:27).

The first healing belongs to those done on the Sabbath; the healing occurs through the words of the

Lord: "Hold thy peace and come out of him." In both cases, the demons ask, "What have we to do with thee?" Previously, the Lord had taught in the synagogue and the congregation "were astonished at his doctrine: for he taught them as one that had authority (*exusian*) and not as the scribes." (Mark 1:27, Luke 4:32)

In the second story, the power of the Lord is portrayed through the prior stilling of the sea (Matthew 8:26, Mark 4:39, Luke 8:24). The demons speak through those who are possessed, as we have said, mostly in the plural; even when they express themselves in the singular, there are several of them (Mark 5:9; Luke 8:30). Those who are possessed behave as if they are asking for help (as in the stories cited in III.2 above), running to the Lord and throwing themselves down before him. But what comes from them is the speech of the demons. Their most striking aspect is their vocal recognition of the Lord. The subconscious formations in the soul couldn't do this on their own. Their capacity means that these otherwise negative forms, these senseless forces, have a connection to the higher element within the possessed person—a connection to the spiritual part that, as a spiritual being, "sees" other spiritual beings, including the Lord. We could put it this way: In our higher being we know everything, we are clairvoyant; in principle we know the whole world, including the spiritual world. But this knowledge is only available to human beings on earth if, through inner work, they raise their consciousness to the level of their own spiritual nature. In the case of those possessed (psychiatric cases) their center is, at least at times, outside the body-feeling experienced by "normal" people. The improper connection to what is above (*improper* because not consciously controlled and established) gives them an openness through which they can express much that remains hidden from normal folk.

The strong connection between those who are mentally ill and the spiritual world has been widely recognized by figures such as Rudolf Steiner down to representatives of the recent anti-psychiatric movement, R. D. Laing and Thomas Szasz. It is just this openness of the mentally ill that offers the possibility of healing or of expelling the soul's powerful independent formations through the word of the Lord. In Him is the Logos, the word-like, cosmic-creative power of God, to which all spirits are subordinate, including unclean spirits. They know that they will be overcome by the Lord, by his Word:

> If thou cast us out, suffer us to go away into the herd of swine. (Matthew 8:31, Mark 5:7, Luke 8:27)

> Art thou come to destroy us? (Mark 1:24, Luke 4:34)

Since the Logos became flesh through John the Baptist's baptism of Jesus at the river Jordan (John 1:14), God's Word lives in Jesus of Nazareth. There is a cognitive capacity that, in Jesus, fully attains to the Logos that lives within him; it is possible for the possessed person, through this same cognition, to build within himself a higher center, and through the presence of the Logos to separate himself from the independent forms of the soul. They are cast off, even if they do not dissolve: hence the warning, in some cases, that the expelled unclean spirit should not return to the person:

When the unclean spirit is gone out of a man, he
walketh through dry places, seeking rest; and finding none, he saith, I will return unto my house
when I came out. (Luke 11:24) (See also Matthew
12:45.)

Because the everyday center is much stronger today,
an independent form within the soul can only very
seldom become dissociated (that is, cast out). Instead, it
must be dissolved or at least transformed into a socially
acceptable form. A subconscious formation can only be
dissolved completely through a counter-intuition.

All cognitive capacity belongs to the true human
being, to his or her higher nature, but it can be used by
the demons. This is similar to our tendency to ascribe the
activities of our higher nature (knowing, sense-perception, thinking, insight, etc.) to the everyday I, since everyday consciousness is the only consciousness to which we
have access without a schooling of consciousness.

In the case of those who are possessed, demons
control the everyday I, which was weaker at the time of
the Lord than it is today. When the demons use words
like "torture, destroy, kill," they mean that they fear
these independent forms will be separated from the
higher self of the person—that is, their parasitic intelligence will be unmasked. And this would mean that
the person becomes free of them. The transformation in
question is portrayed at the end of the expulsion story
in Luke 8:27-39: "Now the man out of whom the devils
were departed besought him that he might be with him:
but Jesus sent him away, saying, Return to thine own
house, and shew how great things God hath done unto
thee. And he went his way, and published throughout the

whole city how great things Jesus had done unto him." The more developed I-body protects us today from these powerful independent entities. Without this, we become vulnerable both to what is below (in the direction of the subconscious) and to what is above. In psychiatric cases, spiritual perceptions and impulses are mixed with the forms of the subconscious.

Pondering 9

How does the I-body protect us?

Meditation 11

"But if I with the finger of God cast out devils, no doubt the kingdom of God is come upon you." (Luke 11:20)

Meditation 12

He cast out spirits with the Word (*Logos*).

IV.

BODILY HEALINGS

The expulsion of demons always happens through the Word of the Lord. Some bodily ailments are also cured through his Word, but in most cases touch seems to play a big role in the process. Touch happens in the form of the laying on of hands, lifting someone up, sometimes anointing the person with saliva, and also often when the sick person touches the Lord or his garment. Outwardly, we can distinguish between three forms of bodily healing: those with touch, those without touch, and those from afar. The last of these are the most spiritually powerful of the healings, so we will examine them first.

IV.1. Healings from Afar through the Word

The story of the centurion (Matthew 8:5, Luke 7:2) or the nobleman (John 4:46) is given this way in Matthew:

> And when Jesus was entered into Capernaum, there came unto him a centurion, beseeching him. And saying, Lord, my servant lieth at home sick of the palsy, grievously tormented. And Jesus saith

unto him, I will come and heal him. The centurion
answered and said, Lord, I am not worthy that
thou shouldest come under my roof: but speak the
word only, and my servant shall be healed. For I
am a man under authority, having soldiers under
me: and I say to this man, Go, and he goeth; and to
another Come, and he cometh; and to my servant,
Do this, and he doeth it. When Jesus heard it, he
marveled, and said to them that followed, Verily I
say unto you, I have not found so great faith, no,
not in Israel.... And Jesus said unto the centurion,
Go thy way; and as thou hast believed, so be it
done unto thee. And his servant was healed in the
selfsame hour.

The essence of both of these healings lies the faith of
the intermediate person and not, as in the majority of
healings, in the faith of the person who is sick. The sick
person may not even know about the process. But someone other than the Lord has to have a special faith—one
that even astonishes the Lord. This special kind of faith
(or certainty) not only enables the Lord to bring healing,
but also enables the Lord's Word to have an effect at a
distance. We can understand this through what the Lord
says when he acknowledges this kind of special faith and
then allows healing to proceed:

Then Jesus answered and said unto her, O woman,
great is thy faith: be it unto thee even as thou wilt.
And her daughter was made whole from that very
hour. (Matthew 15:28) (See also Matthew 8:10;
Luke 7:9; Mark 7:29).

Through the intermediary's faith, the healing *dynamis* or meaningful power can reach the sick person at a distance: they are raised, with the intermediary and the Lord, into a realm of light. That—the knowledge of how this works—is in the background of the special testimonies of certainty: space and time have no bearing on such healings.

The other notable trait in these cases comes to light only in Greek. Where, in German or English, it says "only speak a word," we read *eipe logo*. *Eipein*, in general, means "to say," though what kind of saying depends on the context. For example, it can mean "bless" or the opposite. *Logo* is the dative of logos, a word that means not only "word" but *the* Word, the meaning-making power of God. *Eipe logo* therefore means, not "speak the word," but rather "speak with the power of the Logos." So Jesus' astonishment is much more understandable. The centurion is demonstrating his deep awareness of the power by which the Lord heals.

In the second case of healing at a distance, it is not a question of bodily illness. Here it is according to Matthew (15:22):

> And behold, a woman of Canaan came out of the same coasts, and cried unto him, saying, Have mercy on me, O Lord, thou son of David: my daughter is grievously vexed with a devil. But he answered her not a word. And his disciples came and besought him, saying, Send her away: for she crieth after us. But he answered and said, I am not sent but unto the lost sheep of the house of Israel. Then came she and worshipped him, saying, Lord, help me. But he answered and said, it is not meet

to take the children's bread, and to cast it to dogs. And she said, Truth, Lord: yet the dogs eat of the crumbs which fall from their masters' table. Then Jesus answered and said unto her, O woman, great is thy faith: be it unto thee even as thou wilt. And her daughter was made whole from that very hour.

The same story can be found in Mark 7:25-30:

For a certain woman, whose young daughter had an unclean spirit, heard of him, and came and fell at his feet: The woman was a Greek, a Syrophenician by nation; and she besought him that he would cast forth the devil out of her daughter. But Jesus said unto her, Let the children first be filled: for it is not meet to take the children's bread and to cast it unto the dogs. And she answered and said unto him, Yes, Lord: yet the dogs under the table eat of the children's crumbs. And he said unto her, For this saying go thy way; the devil is gone out of thy daughter. And when she was come to her house, she found the devil gone out and her daughter laid upon the bed.

It is striking here that Jesus at first does not want to help, since the woman is a gentile (pagan). Something similar is spoken to the twelve disciples (Matthew 10:5 ff.):

These twelve Jesus sent forth, and commanded them, saying, Go not into the way of the Gentiles, and into any city of the Samaritans enter ye not: But go rather to the lost sheep of the house of Israel.

"Rather" is not an absolute prohibition. Though it is clearly said "go not into ... any city of the Samaritans," in (Luke 9:52) the Lord allows them to "enter ... into a village of the Samaritans, to make ready for him"; the good Samaritan (Luke 10:33) has become a byword; from the ten lepers, only one turned to thank the Lord (Luke 17:16): "And fell down on his face at his feet, giving him thanks: and he was a Samaritan." In the fourth chapter of John we read about a long, profound discussion with a Samaritan woman. And in the Acts of the Apostles (Chapter 8), we hear nothing of such a prohibition.

The outer appearance of a human being, like every phenomenon perceptible to the senses, is the sign of a "meaning"—of the person's "mission"—for which he or she came to earth. Every human being has such a "mission," though it cannot be put into words. When we turn within ourselves with intense feeling-attentiveness, we can sense at any moment whether or not we are acting in line with our mission. Illnesses are signs that we have lost the direction of our mission; they are warnings, so that we can find our way back. The Lord's healings all take place accordingly; this is why there often arises some resistance or attempt at avoidance, as for example, in the healing by the lake of Bethesda (John: 5). The healings originate in the sphere of meanings, not in the sphere of signs, of phenomena. Signs (which can be spoken or written) change as meanings change, and it is these meanings that the healings affect. The human environment sees the healed signs. In the spiritual world of meanings there is no space (no distance) and also no time (the healings almost all occur immediately); this is why healing can happen at a distance. Through the intermediary's consciousness, the *dynamis* or the healing, meaning-bearing power of the Lord "finds" the sick person. The person is, after all, connected with the intermediary's soul, present in their consciousness, and so accessible to the Lord, who knows the thoughts and feelings of those around him. The intermediary's faith opens the way, is the way, for the Lord's healing power to reach the sick person.

Some of the healings in the Gospels take place neither at a distance nor by touch. At times, the Lord heals both illnesses of the soul and also physical illnesses through his Word. This is what happens with the man sick of the "palsy" who, according to Mark (2:3) and Luke (5:18) is lowered down through the open roof to Jesus. (Matthew (9:2) does not mention this detail). Here is Mark (2:3):

> And they come unto him, bringing one sick of the palsy, which was borne of four. And when they could not come nigh unto him for the press, they uncovered the roof where he was: and when they had broken it up, they let down the bed wherein the sick of the palsy lay. When Jesus saw their faith, he said unto the sick of the palsy, Son, thy sins be forgiven thee. But there were certain of the scribes sitting there, and reasoning in their hearts, Why doth this man thus speak blasphemies? who can forgive sins but God only? And immediately when Jesus perceived in his spirit that they so reasoned within themselves, he said unto them: Why reason ye these things in your hearts? Whether is it easier to say to the sick of the palsy, Thy sins be forgiven thee; or to say, Arise and take up they bed, and walk? But that ye may know that the Son of Man hath power on earth to forgive sins (he saith to the

sick of the palsy), I say unto thee, Arise, and take up thy bed, and go thy way into thine house. And immediately he arose, took up the bed, and went forth before them all; insomuch that they were all amazed, and glorified God, saying: We never saw it on this fashion.

The address "Son" (like "Daughter" in the story of the woman with an issue of blood) shows how Jesus felt toward the man who was sick. We can assume that those who are suffering could not, in terms of their age, be the son or daughter of Jesus, who would have been about thirty years old. But in respect of the Logos dwelling within him, all men and women are his sons and daughters. Being freed from sins "on earth" suggests the momentary distancing from the "me" or the separating robe, the lower human. The higher self, now outside and independent of the body, can obey the word of the Lord: "Arise..." There follows, "go...into thine house" (often translated as "home"), but "house" in the New Testament generally means the everyday consciousness out of which the sick person is released during the healing.[14]

In Luke, the story is almost the same as in Mark, while in Matthew it is slightly different, and lacks the "I say unto you." This expression underlines the I-ness of the healing, which takes place openly at mid-day and before many witnesses, in contrast to the many healings of the time that were performed in a special, non-waking consciousness. What "amazed" the witnesses is this trait: the openness of the healings. "I say unto you" would be logically unnecessary, and in Greek even the word "I" is unnecessary, being built into the form of the verb, and so its explicit use supports the wakeful understanding of what is being said. We also find this phrase in the story of the widow's son in Nain (Luke 7:14) and in the case of Jairus' daughter (Mark 4:41).

Another healing through the Word belongs to the Sabbath events, in which the Lord uses the holiness of the day for the sake of healing. It brings him into conflict with the scribes, who consider all work on the Sabbath to be forbidden. The healing takes place in the synagogue, therefore in public once again. A man with a withered hand becomes the test case between Jesus and the scribes and Pharisees (Matthew 12:6; Mark 3:1; Luke 6:6). In Mark (from 2:27):

> And he said unto them, The sabbath was made for man, and not man for the sabbath. Therefore the Son of man is Lord also of the sabbath. And he entered again into the synagogue; and there was a man there which had a withered hand. And they watched him, whether he would heal him on the sabbath day; that they might accuse him. And he saith unto the man who had the withered hand, Stand forth. And he saith unto them, Is it lawful to do good on the sabbath days, or to do evil? to save life, or to kill? But they held their peace. And when he had looked round about on them with anger, being grieved for the hardness of their hearts, he saith unto the man, Stretch forth thine hand. And he stretched it out: and his hand was restored whole as the other. And the Pharisees went forth, and straightway took counsel with the Herodians against him, how they might destroy him.

After the healing, the Pharisees and scribes are filled with anoia or senselessness—"madness" in the King James version (6:11). Apart from not being able to bear the living, effective spirituality, the public nature of the miraculous deed done by Jesus was also a thorn in their sides. But this is the fundamental characteristic of the New Testament: the tendency to un-hiddenness;[15] that is, what earlier could only occur in secret is to be brought into the light by Christianity (Matthew 10:26; Luke 12:2). The man with the withered hand seems quite passive in this story, but we can guess that when he steps into their midst, hope and faith in healing blossom within him. In the discussion of healing (Mark 9:24), it is clear that the presence of an "open" being, like Jesus, for whom the heavens are open, also renders them open to others, just as openness to the superconscious heaven of one's own soul induces something similar in others.

The healing of the blind beggar Bartimaeus (Mark 10:46, Luke 18:35) also takes place through the Word. According to Mark:

> And they came to Jericho: and as he went out of Jericho with his disciples and a great number of people, blind Bartimaeus, the son of Timaeus, sat by the highway side begging. And when he heard that it was Jesus of Nazareth, he began to cry out, and say, Jesus, thou son of David, have mercy on me. And many charged him that he should hold his peace; but he cried the more a great deal, Thou son of David, have mercy on me. And Jesus stood still, and commanded him to be called. And they call the blind man, saying unto him, Be of good

comfort, rise; he calleth thee. And he rose, casting away his garment, rose, and came to Jesus. And Jesus answered and said unto him, What wilt thou that I should do unto thee? The blind man said unto him, Lord, that I might receive my sight. And Jesus said unto him, Go thy way; thy faith hath made thee whole. And immediately he received his sight, and followed Jesus in the way.

Like the woman of Canaan, the blind men who are healed recognize Jesus as the son of David. Because the visible signs are not there to distract them, they "see" the essential nature of the Lord, the Messiah. The expression "made thee whole," or "saved thee," is *sozo* in Greek and means "make healthy, preserve, save, free, redeem." As a healer, the Lord is called *soter*, based on the same verb. *Soteria* means "preservation, saving, certainty." And what becomes "he received his sight" in the King James translation comes originally from the Greek word *anablepein*, which means "to look upward." This is how it is used in the miracle of the loaves (Matthew 14:19; Luke 9,10 and Mark 6:41):

And when he had taken the five loaves and the two fishes, he looked up to heaven, and blessed, and brake the loaves...

and again in another healing, when the Lord looks up to heaven (Matthew 7:34). If we meditate on the cases of healing those who are blind, we need to consider this nuance. Besides Bartimaeus, there are other blind people who are healed (Matthew 9:27; 20:29) when their eyes are touched. The two lepers already referred to are healed without touch (Luke 17:11):

> And when he saw them he said unto them, go shew yourselves unto the priests. And it came to pass, that, as they went, they were cleansed.

Meditation 13

Speak by the Logos, with the Logos-power. (*eipe logo*)

Meditation 14

(I) say unto you, arise, take up thy bed, and go to your own house.

IV.2. Healings through Touch

Those who are sick may be healed through the touch of the Lord, even by touching his garment. In Matthew (14:35):

> And when the men of that place [Genasareth] had knowledge of him, they sent out into all that country round about, and brought unto him all that were diseased; And besought him that they might only touch the hem of his garment; and as many as touched were made perfectly whole.

Luke (6:19) describes something similar:

> And the whole multitude sought to touch him: for there went virtue out of him, and healed them all.

The Lord mentions this power or virtue in the story of the woman with an issue of blood (Mark 5:30) when she touches his garment and is healed:

> And Jesus, immediately knowing in himself that virtue had gone out of him....

In these portrayals, the word "virtue" is expressed in Greek by *dynamis*. This word means, along with power or force, the power of movement and meaning. For example, you could say that the meaning of a sentence is the power or virtue (*dynamis*). It is not a blind, formless force that goes out from the Lord. It is meaningful: it restores the meaningful form of the sick body-part and also restores the possibility of a meaningful life. It shifts the healed person in the direction of his or her individual earthly mission, giving life its new (and original) meaning.

Through touch, a leper is healed in Matthew 8:2; Mark 1:40; and Luke 5:12. According to Mark:

> And there came a leper to him, beseeching him, and kneeling down to him, and saying unto him, If thou wilt, thou canst make me clean. And Jesus, moved with compassion, put forth his hand, and touched him, and saith unto him, I will; be thou clean. And as soon as he had spoken, immediately the leprosy departed from him, and he was cleansed.

The *dynamis* is itself form-free, and so this power can reinstate forms. In the awakening of the dead youth of Nain (Luke 7:14), the Lord touches the coffin where the dead man lies. The three synoptic gospels tell the story of the healing of Peter's mother-in-law (Matthew 8:14, Luke 4:38). In Mark (1:30) we read:

> But Simon's wife's mother lay sick of a fever, and anon they tell him of her. And he came and took her by the hand, and lifted her up; and immediately the fever left her, and she ministered unto them.

We can also find stories in the Gospels in which the healing does not take place through simple touch, but through the application of substances. For example, the healing of the deaf mute (Mark 7:32):

> And he took him aside from the multitude, and he put his fingers into his ears, and he spit, and touched his tongue; And straightway his ears were opened, and the string of his tongue was loosed, and he spake plain.

The gradual healing of a blind man, like that of the man born blind (John 9:6), goes beyond simple touch (Mark 8:23):

> And he took the blind man by the hand, and led him out of the town; and when he had spit on his eyes, and put his hands upon him, he asked him if he saw ought. And he looked up, and said, I see men as trees, walking. After that he put his hands again upon his eyes, and made him look up: and he was restored, and saw every man clearly.

The healing of the aged, crippled woman (Luke 13:11) occurs through a laying on of hands, on the Sabbath:

And behold, there was a woman which had a spirit of infirmity eighteen years, and was bowed together, and could in no wise lift up herself. And when Jesus saw her, he called her to him, and said unto her, Woman, thou art loosed from thine infirmity. And he laid his hands on her; and immediately she was made straight, and glorified God.

The last healing concerns the servant Malchus' ear, cut off by Peter's sword at the time of Christ's arrest (Mark 14:47, Matthew 26:51). Peter's name is mentioned only in John (18:10); the healing in question, a healing through touch, is told only in Luke (22:51):

And Jesus answered and said Suffer ye thus far. And he touched his ear, and healed him.

What is the role of touch during the healings? Faith is the precondition for a *dynamis* going from the Lord to the sick person who touches him. Nothing similar happens during an accidental touch, as we can tell from the story of Jairus' daughter and the connected story of the woman with the issue of blood. When the Lord touches the sick person himself, it can have an additional significance. Particularly in the case of Jairus' daughter, with Peter's mother-in-law, and with lepers, it may be that touch has the function of drawing the healed person, their spiritual essence, back into the body, since the act of touching makes them feel the body directly. For the healing itself always takes place when the spiritual essence is lifted "outside," that is, independent of the body, and raised into the light, the form-free sphere of light. This is certainly so in the case of the healed child (Mark 9:26), that lies as if dead after an unclean spirit is driven from him: the Lord takes the child's hand and raises him on his legs.

> And the spirit cried, and rent him sore, and came out of him: and he was as one dead; insomuch that many said, He is dead. But Jesus took him by the hand, and lifted him up; and he arose.

We can guess that often both the functions of touch are active when the Lord initiates the touching.

Meditation 15

I will. Be thou cleansed.

IV.3. *Individual Healings*

In this section we will consider certain healings that are described in detail and so acquire a special importance.

1. *The Impotent Man at Bethesda (John 5:2)*

> After this there was a feast of the Jews; and Jesus went up to Jerusalem. Now there is at Jerusalem by the sheep market a pool, which is called in the Hebrew tongue Bethesda, having five porches. In these lay a great multitude of impotent folk, of blind, halt, withered, waiting for the moving of the water. For an angel went down at a certain season into the pool, and troubled the water: whosoever then first after the troubling of the water stepped in was made whole of whatsoever disease he had. And a certain man was there, which had an infirmity thirty and eight years. When Jesus saw him

lie, and knew that he had been now a long time in that case, he saith unto him, Wilt thou be made whole? The impotent man answered him, Sir, I have no man, when the water is troubled, to put me into the pool: but while I am coming, another steppeth down before me. Jesus saith unto him, Rise, take up thy bed, and walk. And immediately the man was made whole, and took up his bed, and walked: and on the same day was the sabbath.

Jesus' question is, "Do you want to be made whole?"— a passive grammatical construction. Since he knows how long the man has been waiting, it is evident that the question is not about the everyday will, as in, "Would you like to...?" Rather, it is addressed to the primal will of the human being: the decision as to the individual mission with which, and through which, every human being comes to earth. He is saying, "Do you have the primal will that, if it is not lost, admits of no illness?"

The word "healthy," or "well," or "whole," means living in the direction of one's primal mission; if you do, no illness can approach you. The answer of the sick man here shows that he does not understand the question; he is speaking out of his everyday consciousness and avoids the question. He neither dares to say, nor can he say, "I will"—not even in terms of everyday consciousness. We have the impression that he actually does not want to alter his situation; he clings to it; the habit-man within him is strong and admits of no change, for every change means risk, and the situation as it has been for 38 years, though painful and unsatisfying, is also familiar and "safe." If he were to be healed, then his life would be altered in dramatic, unforeseen, risky ways. If we are honest, we would have to answer the Lord's question with a shame-faced but definite "No." And that is just what the sick man does, though not openly. If nothing further happened, no healing would take place. But through being addressed, the fundamental orientation of his soul was externalized, made objective, and so his soul could confront it.

Something then took place without words, and therefore does not find its way into the text. If we put this wordless event into words (which can of course only provide a hint at the inner change of direction, the shift in feeling), it might go like this: "O God, what have I said? How inadequate was my answer! It is not my innermost being that spoke just then. My God and my Lord, forgive what I have said and yes, I will it, I say yes to being healed, to change, to life." Horror at what he has said opens the man up. "What have I done?"— a question that does not apply to the present moment alone, but reaches back through his whole past—not in biographical details, but in the realm of feeling, and this feeling-flame may burn its way back through earlier lives, even all the way to Paradise. For to be healed, we have to be led back before the Fall; every illness we experience now dates from that point.

Through this kind of retrospective self-examination, which takes place not in consciousness, but in a super-conscious feeling, the sick person is healed. Then Jesus, having perceived this wordless transformation, says to him, "Arise..." And it happens. "Take up thy bed" occurs in other healings too, for example Mark 2:11, Matthew 9:6, Luke 5:24, in the healing of the lame man. The meaning of this action could be (though, again, the words only suggest a direction in which to think or feel about it): "Don't let your past, your former home-base, just lie there. What you lay on, what carried you, is now for you to carry: grow active toward it." Jesus does not speak a healing word to this sick man (such as, "Thy sins are forgiven"), but tells him what he should do after or since he is already healed, and can stand up, and can walk.

The story of the pool at Bethesda takes place on a Sabbath, the day on which no one should carry a bed. But *that* is merely a pretext. The healing took place in full public view (5:13), and that was the real scandal.

The postscript begins with Verse 13:

> And he that was healed wist not who it was; for Jesus had conveyed himself away, a multitude being in that place. Afterward Jesus findeth him in the temple, and said unto him, Behold, thou art made whole: sin no more, lest a worse thing come unto thee. The man departed, and told the Jews that it was Jesus, which had made him whole.

The healing happens outside ordinary consciousness— for an instant. Before, as well as afterward, the healed man is in his everyday consciousness. He is asked, he answers, and afterward he does as Jesus tells him. When Jesus speaks to him in the Temple, he recognizes his healer. And now something like a relapse happens to the man. Jesus' warning words, "lest a worse thing come unto thee," allow us to guess: Jesus saw the man was in danger. Instead of following his healer, he reports to the scribes who it was who suggested he carry his bed.

Meditation 16

Wilt thou be made whole?

2. *The Story of the Father*

This story of the father of the man with a "dumb spirit" is perhaps the most human of the healings Mark (9:17):

> And one of the multitude answered and said, Master, I have brought unto thee my son, which hath a dumb spirit; And wheresoever he taketh him, he teareth him: and he foameth, and gnasheth with his teeth, and pineth away; and I spake to thy disciples that they should cast him out; and they could not. He answereth him, and saith, O faithless generation, how long shall I be with you? how long shall I suffer you? bring him unto me. And they brought him unto Him: and when He saw him, straightway the spirit tare him; and he fell on the ground, and wallowed foaming. And He asked his father, How long is it ago since this came unto him? And he said, Of a child. And oftimes it hath cast him into the fire, and into the waters, to destroy him: but if thou canst do any thing, have compassion on us, and help us. Jesus saith unto him, If thou canst? all things are possible to him that believeth. And straightway the father of the child cried out, and said with tears, Lord, I believe; help thou mine unbelief. When Jesus saw that the people came running together, he rebuked the foul spirit, saying unto him, Thou dumb and deaf spirit, I charge thee, come out of him, and enter no more into him. And the spirit cried, and rent him sore, and came out of him: and he was as one dead; insomuch that many said, He is dead. But Jesus took him by the hand, and lifted him up; and he arose.

The father is disappointed that the disciples cannot heal his child. Now he is also unsure if Jesus can: "If thou canst do anything..." Our sources give us Jesus' answer in different ways; the likeliest version is, "If thou canst?"—that is, repeating the father's words with a smile, the only place in the New Testament where we can imagine a smile. And the father is the kind of person Jesus could address this way, making it a very human kind of dialogue.

Then the story grows more emotional. After Jesus' words to the father that "all things are possible to him that believeth," the father recognizes who he is dealing with. What happens next takes place without words, just as in the case of the sick man at the pool of Bethesda. What have I said? What have I done? A review through this life, through the preceding life, back to Paradise. In tears, he calls aloud, "I believe!" Certainty flashes forth in him and immediately dies out again into, "Help thou mine unbelief." This sentence is itself the salvation. For he "sees" his own unbelief and at the same time believes that he can be helped; he believes in this help. He "knows," too, that his son's healing depends on this, and that two who believe must always be present for healing to occur. With this, he opens himself up—though the fear that his son could go unhealed contributes to the opening as well—to the influence of the primal Openness, and it induces in him that great openness we call certainty or faith. It is not only certainty that the healing will be successful, but the absolute conviction that could be expressed as follows: everything is all right, meaningful; grace is ever-present. The father's uncertainty (*apistia*) is healed, and therefore his son is healed.

Meditation 17

Help thou mine unbelief (uncertainty).

3. *The Healing of the Man Born Blind*

This healing is characteristic of the Lord's healing activity for very different reasons. The story and its aftermath are very fully described, and they continually return to the theme of light in John (9:1):

> And as Jesus passed by, he saw a man which was blind from his birth. And his disciples asked him, saying, Master, who did sin, this man, or his parents, that he was born blind? Jesus answered, Neither hath this man sinned, nor his parents: but that the works of God should be made manifest in him. I must work the works of him that sent me, while it is day: the night cometh, when no man can work. As long as I am in the world, I am the light of the world. When he had thus spoken, he spat on the ground, and made clay of the spittle, and he anointed the eyes of the blind man with the clay, and said unto him, Go, wash in the pool of Siloam (which is by interpretation, Sent.) He went his way therefore, and washed, and came seeing. The neighbors therefore, and they which before had seen him that he was blind, said, Is not this he that sat and begged? Some said, This is he: others said, he is like him: but he said, I am.

From the disciples' initial question it is clear that reincarnation was something obvious and accepted among them. Jesus' answer to their question shows that a congenital weakness such as blindness need not be conditioned by the past, but can have a completely different meaning: for example, to instill one's neighbors with a certain impulse, or to make manifest the inner divine kernel of a person—as in this story.

The walk to the pool of Siloam secures or tests the faith of the blind man: he has to have a lasting certainty. He has to be present the whole long way, not simply in a momentary flash, but all the way to the place where he can wash his eyes in the water. By saying "I am," the healed man (the only one besides the Lord in the New Testament who says *ego eimi*, I AM) means: every I AM is the light of the world; in every such being the world wakes to full awareness and receives its meaning. And this is independent of the past. Jesus' words of self-disclosure in John (9:37) gain significance when we can distinguish between the speaker and the bodily phenomenon, as we are urged to do:[16]

> And Jesus said unto him, Thou hast both seen him [the Son of God] and it is he that talketh with thee.

The man born blind has "seen" him during the healing, hence the *praeterite* or past tense form of the verb. He is standing in front of the Lord now, after all, and sees him with his physical eyes, but Jesus is not talking about this kind of sight.

> For judgment I am come into this world, that they which see not might see; and that they which see might be made blind. (John 9:39)

> If ye were blind, ye should have no sin: but now
> ye say, We see; therefore your sin remaineth. (John
> 9:41).

Jesus' words to the Pharisees at the end of the chapter express something that relates to every human being: Measured by or compared with what we could see (what we could know) if we developed our capacities for understanding, we are all blind.

Meditation 18

I am the light of the world.

4. *The Daughter of Jairus and the Woman with an Issue of Blood*

This healing is given, with insignificant variations, in all three synoptic Gospels (Matthew 9:18; Mark 5:22: Luke 8:41). In Mark we read:

> And, behold, there cometh one of the rulers of the
> synagogue, Jairus, by name; and when he saw him,
> he fell at his feet. And besought him greatly, saying,
> My little daughter lieth at the point of death: I
> pray thee, come and lay thy hands on her, that she
> may be healed; and she shall live. And Jesus went
> with him; and much people followed him, and
> thronged him. And a certain woman, which had
> an issue of blood twelve years, and had suffered
> many things of many physicians, and had spent all
> that she had, and was nothing bettered, but rather
> grew worse. When she had heard of Jesus, came
> in the press behind, and touched his garment. For

she said, If I may touch but his clothes, I shall be whole. And straightway the fountain of her blood was dried up; and she felt in her body that she was healed of that plague. And Jesus, immediately knowing in himself that virtue had gone out of him, turned him about in the press, and said, Who touched my clothes? And his disciples said unto him, Thou seest the multitude thronging thee, and sayest thou, who touched me? And he looked round about to see her that had done this thing. But the woman fearing and trembling, knowing what was done to her, came and fell down before him, and told him all the truth. And he said unto her, Daughter, thy faith hath made thee whole; go in peace, and be whole of thy plague. While he yet spake, there came from the ruler of the synagogue's house certain which said, Thy daughter is dead: why troublest thou the Master further? As soon as Jesus heard the word that was spoken, he saith unto the ruler of the synagogue, Be not afraid, only believe. And he suffered no man to follow him, save Peter, and James, and John the brother of James. And he cometh to the house of the ruler of the synagogue, and seeth the tumult, and them that wept and wailed greatly. And when he was come in, he saith unto them, Why make ye this ado, and weep? The damsel is not dead, but sleepeth. And they laughed him to scorn. But when he had put them all out, he taketh the father and the mother of the damsel, and them that were with him, and entereth in where the damsel was lying. And he took the damsel by the hand, and said unto her, Talitha cumi; which is, being interpreted,

Damsel, I say unto thee, arise. And straightway the damsel arose, and walked; for she was of the age of twelve years.

In this story, two healings go together. First the woman with the issue of blood is healed. From her mere touch, Jesus feels that virtue, dynamis, goes forth from him, though he was surrounded by many people. It is not the physical touch that counts, but the faith: the touch was the sign rather than the meaning. He addresses the woman as "daughter," which couldn't be right in terms of her age. Rather, this form of address is like an echo of the father's words at the beginning of the story. Both of those who are healed are called "daughter." The one has an excess of blood, the other stands just before the age of puberty. After hearing the report that she is dead, the Lord utters the seminal words (v. 36): Do not fear, only believe. What is required is certainty—both in general and in regard to the awakening of the child. He means that without the father's faith the daughter could not be brought back from death. His faith is the magical background, like the painter's canvas, on which the awakening appears like the picture. The atmosphere of certainty, of complete conviction that the event will occur, without the slightest shadow of doubt—all this is included in an absolute certainty. The bearer of the Word is present, of course, and that helps.

Meditation 19

If I could but touch his garment, I would be healed.

Meditation 20

Fear not, only believe.

5. Healing the Blind

Healings of the blind resemble the healing of Bartimeus, though in that case there is no reference to touching the eyes (Mark 10:46; Luke 18:35). Otherwise, almost everything is word for word the same. The healings take place in the neighborhood of Jericho; the Lord asks what the blind people want him to do to them; after the healing they follow him. It does not seem essential that in Matthew (20:29-34) two blind men are mentioned, instead of just one; we encountered something similar in the expulsion of demons. The fourth healing of a blind person takes place near Nazareth in Matthew (9:27). There are, once again, two beggars, who don't even say what they want, they merely ask for mercy. Without their expressing their wish, as in other healings, the Lord asks them, "Believe ye that I am able to do this?" After their affirmation, the Lord touches their eyes: "Be it done unto you according to your faith." In Mark and Luke, no touch is mentioned, only in the two stories in Matthew. All those who are blind address the Lord as the Son of David. This is what the "people" guess at after a particular healing:

> Then was brought unto him one possessed with a devil, blind, and dumb: and he healed him, insomuch that the blind and dumb both spake and saw. And all the people were amazed, and said, Is not this the son of David? (Matthew 12:22-23)

After the Lord's entry into Jerusalem, this guess becomes a certainty (Matthew 21:9).

And the multitudes that went before, and that followed, cried, saying Hosanna to the Son of David: Blessed is he that cometh in the name of the Lord...

The disparity among the accounts be reconciled through the meditative encounter with the "material." In meditation, the essence of the theme—healing the blind—becomes experiential: the faith, the necessity of expressing one's wish, even the recognition of the Messiah ("Son of David"). But meditation also, in its light, suggests that humanity will return to a state of *seeing* by way of this detour through faith or certainty as the relationship of humankind and the Godhead in early Christianity. We will return to "seeing"—to the direct experience of spirit, as indicated through the healings of those who are blind, even the man born blind.

Meditation 21

What will you that I do unto you? That our eyes may be opened.

IV.4. *The Language of Healing*

In the case of both spoken and written language, the visible or audible part is completed by our inner activity. In speaking or writing, this inner activity determines the outwardly apparent part; in hearing or reading, the apparent part leads us toward understanding through a parallel inner activity.[17] In both cases, the two sides of language match one another, like the shaded and unshaded parts of a circle.

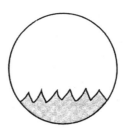

The shaded part of this circle represents the apparent part, the sign-side of language (words and grammar); the unshaded part symbolizes the corresponding inner activity (meaning). In different languages, the apparent part may be larger or smaller in relation to the meaning part. Languages that are poor in words and grammar demand a deeper inner activity of intuition. The extreme case would be a silent primal language, primal communication, where the beings are themselves communication in a spiritual world, where no signs are exchanged, but only meanings. To be sure, these would be higher meanings than those we normally conceive. Following are two texts by Rudolf Steiner: the first describes the style of communication in the spiritual world and the second characterizes the language of the Lord during his healings.

CW 231, November 14, 1923:

> What the human being expresses, what passes into our fleeting words, would be, at the same time, a self-expression of the whole person—at the same

time the essence and the revelation of the person. There you have an image of how, between death and a new birth, one human being meets another, distinguishing among themselves and revealing themselves. Word meets word; articulated word meets articulated word; inwardly enlivened word meets inwardly enlivened word. But the people are these words; their encounter is the resonance of their articulated word-natures. They live without opacity: they truly live *with* each other, and the one word, which is the one person, opens up within the other word, which is the other person. There the fateful connections are formed that remain through the next lifetime on earth, and that manifest in the sympathy and antipathy people feel when they meet. This feeling is a reflection of how they addressed each other in the spiritual world in between death and their new birth. That is how we spoke with each other when we ourselves were speech—our feelings for each other on earth are a mere shadowy reflection of it.

Being in the spiritual world becomes superconscious capacity here on earth. For the elements of communication through signs also originate in the superconscious: the birth of what you want to say, the finding of the words, the work of the speech-organs.

Steiner speaks about the language used in the New Testament's healings in CW 175, a lecture given on April 10, 1917:

Outwardly, Christ Jesus had to express himself in the language of those who were listening to him.

But what he had before his soul in the way of an inward word did not correspond to the way words in a language are formed outwardly. Rather, it had within it the lost power of the Word, the undifferentiated power of speech. We need to form an idea of this power, which is independent of the various differentiated languages, and which lives in a human being when the Word completely permeates our spirit. Otherwise we cannot rise to the level of the power that lived in Christ, nor can we know what it means to speak of Christ as the "Word." It was with this that he had completely identified, and it was through this that he worked when he did his healings and cast out demons. This Word had to be lost, as part of human evolution since the Mystery of Golgotha. But now the Word has to be sought again. For the moment, however, we are in a period of development in which it does not seem likely that we will find our way back to it.

We have to distinguish between the "undifferentiated power of speech" and the signless communication by which meanings can be apprehended without mediation. In the case of the young child during language acquisition, the meanings in the adults' consciousness are formulated in a specific language. The "undifferentiated power of speech," however, the inner word of the Lord, was not the inner complement of the outward signs he used that belonged to a particular language. Rather, it was the creative primal language that had not yet broken into signs or even into the meanings of a language. In this sense, his often-used formula "I say unto you," gains an extraordinary significance.

Pondering 10

When does a text *have an effect* (as if automatically) in everyday life?

Meditation 22

To become whole (healthy) is to *grow* healthy.

Meditation 23

Words protect thinking from dissolution.

Meditation 24

In the spiritual world, nothing separates beings.

When *we* say, "Your sins are forgiven," the people we address will not be able to perceive much of a change in their nature. They would have to realize such a sentence in their own meditation, if they can. That would be the precondition for healing: lifting oneself out of the "flesh" and into one's own spirituality, which is unseparated from the Lord. The words of an initiate, such as Moses or Bodhidharma, would make the process easier through the heightened awareness of the speaker, not through the form of the sounds that they might utter but through the presence, the being of the speaker behind the spoken signs. In such cases, the signs are *full*, spoken and understood in their primal meaning rather than in one of their applied, everyday meanings. If the Lord speaks—the incarnate Logos, living in the undifferentiated power of language, identical with it, God's creative Word—then the elevation of awareness comes not from the perception of the vocalized signs, but through the presence, the radiance (*gloria*, *doxa*, glory) of the Logos-being: the sentence is realized. And with it the healing—the restitution of one's capacity to live according to the meaning of one's individual life—which is never expressible in words. It is like a moment's return to Paradise before the Fall. Yet, this can now occur with self-awareness, in a higher consciousness of the Self. It is called the Kingdom of Heaven, or of God.

Meditation 25

The kingdom of God can only be seen after the expulsion from Paradise.

V.

GOSPEL HEALINGS
IN THE LIGHT OF ANTHROPOSOPHY

V.1. Introduction

To "understand" the healings in the New Testament, that is, even to be able to follow their course (since we can truly understand them only in meditation) we have to describe and understand the human form very differently from how it is presented in the simplified, popularized version of Steiner's work. The model of "physical body, etheric body, astral body, I" ignores the way in which Steiner uses these terms completely differently in different contexts. Although the fine distinction between, for example, the astral man and the astral body can be found early in his work (CW 45), he often uses the expression "body" even for forces that have become free of the "bodies" or that were never bound in forms at all.

In regard to "bodies" and elsewhere, Rudolf Steiner often uses expressions that suggest spatial images and relationships. Yet in important passages he warns against them, as for instance in the 1918 Afterword to CW 17 (see Appendix 1).

The third issue that has to be mentioned here concerns the dual form of the human being. CW 17 shows that this idea belonged early on to Steiner's viewpoint, as we also see in the even earlier lectures of CW 93a (Appendix 2). All the "members" of the human being have two parts: the spiritual being, the source of spiritual qualities on earth, remains in the spiritual world during our earthly life; what we experience on earth is only a "segment" of the whole human being, really a mirror image of the "upper" human being, who lives on in the spirit (Appendix 3).

The fourth problem concerns Steiner's manner of expression, and the way he changes his descriptions of the relationship between "etheric" and "astral." All *sharp* distinctions lead to misunderstanding. As early as in CW 9 (*Theosophy*), in the chapter on the nature of the human being, he writes, "We could also say that a part of the etheric body is finer that the rest, and this finer part of the etheric body forms a unity with the sentient soul, while the coarser part forms a unity with the physical body" (Appendix 4).

The apparent contradictions in Steiner's texts are in most cases easy to resolve when we consider that he never used a consistent terminology. He counts on the reader or listener to understand from the context rather than to cling to individual words.

V.2. *The Higher Human Being and the Free Forces*

The motto of this theme could be (from CW 17, Chapter IV): "The spiritual world will be designated here as the upper world, the sensory world as the lower." With this, we approach the expression of St. John in his Gospel:

"from above" and "from below" as used in John 2:1. The human being consists in an upper and a lower trinity; after birth, both are present, and the task or effort of the lower human is to make the higher trinity more and more conscious, to experience it consciously, for it is the super-conscious being of the human. Steiner almost always uses the expression "body" with regard to this higher human being, even though it consists exclusively in free, that is, form-free forces. Our essence as *capacities*, that is, our higher selves, cannot be "formed" into "bodies." In everyday consciousness, our capacities are never experienced, but only their products; for example, we experience thoughts but not the thinking process, about which we know nothing (Appendix 5).

The higher human being is linked with the lower at conception, and then even more strongly connected at birth. This higher human consists in free forces of willing, feeling and thinking that are helpful and necessary for our spiritual core as it approaches our lower part. The lower human consists, at least up to birth, in "bodies" that are formed from the same forces as those that are available in the upper human in a form-free state. Everything that the child does *not* inherit comes from above: this includes the communicative bodily movements (eye contact, smiling, standing upright, walking, speaking) and the specifically human, non-bodily capacities (cognitive or imitative will, cognitive feeling, thinking, sense-perception, creative capacities). Of course, it is only in a healthy human environment that all the non-inherited capacities can come into play; they would not develop, for example, in a so-called "wild child" raised by wolves.

Immediately after birth, forces start to be freed from out of the lower human being, out of the formed "bodies." From the life-body, forces of thinking and mental picturing are freed; from the soul-body there come forces of free or cognitive feeling; from the physical body come free forces of will. Steiner's seven-year cycles or life-rhythms are milestones in this process, which continues until death. At death, all the forces are freed from the bodies. We can see that the specifically human capacities permeate the lower human from out of the higher human by the fact that all our capacities remain superconscious, as do the corresponding bodily movements. We don't know, for instance, what our speech organs are doing while we speak. Of course, we also don't know what our muscles are doing when we play tennis, but we do know what our arm is doing, or should do; in speaking, we don't know anything parallel about the movements of the speech organs, nor do we need to know. The sense of our own movement is absent during communicative use of the body, as in mime, sign-language, etc.

The free forces from above, as well as those from below that are becoming free, are what make us educable, capable of self-development, of evolution, of change—in contrast to the natural world (Appendix 6).

Through the free forces from above and from below, the higher and lower aspects of the human being grow together. The forces that become free are available for the use of the higher spiritual being. This is why all communicative activities take place through a spiritual spontaneity that we can also call the soft will. The forces that become free from the lower human being can move the body in a communicative way; for non-communicative movements, proprioception has to develop as the precondition for all the bodily senses (life-sense, sense of movement, sense of balance, sense of touch and warmth).

To keep the free forces free they must be used— as forces of understanding, of love, of creativity, of intelligence.

V.3. Origin of the I-body. The Mirror Image

In Chapter I.2 we described the I-body (see note 2) or lower human being phenomenologically. It is, of course, a form within consciousness, rather than being simply identical with the body. The link between the spiritual essence and the inherited body is already present from conception, but the further grasp of the body by the spiritual essence so that it can move the body, use it, reveal itself in the body directly—all this takes place after birth in two clearly marked stages. The first was described briefly in Chapter V.2 as the communicative use of the body. The link itself can be called "attention," as long as we take this term in a broad enough sense, so that attention can appear as will, feeling, thinking, perception, etc. For no activity, whether inner or outer, takes place without attention. The small child's attention is different from a "normal" adult's attention in that the adult experiences the world dualistically: I am here and the world is there. The child only gradually attains this distinction between self and other. We could say that it initially experiences everything in non-dualistic identity, and it is doubtful whether we can even call it experience at all. For experience means that something is happening to me or in me and that I know about it—which is at the very least questionable in the case of complete identity. In Chapter I.2 we mentioned that it is possible to distinguish, in the stream of attention, between an identifying component and a witnessing component. In spiritual science, these are called astrality and the true I or Self.

The technical term "astral" originally refers to the capacity, or possibility, of identifying all the way to the world of the stars—meaning not the physically visible stars, but the spiritual meanings whose signs they are (Appendix 7).

The separating "robe" arises initially from out of an astrality that is form-free and able to identify with an object. A part of this astrality shapes itself into the first meaningless form (Appendix 8), in which the Self is not present. The separated-off astrality, feeling itself as a form, then "identifies" with itself, and retains a kind of I-ness as the kernel of the I-body, because it serves as a mirror for the Self. Since the Self is not self-aware, it confuses itself with this mirror image (Appendix 9).

We could also express it this way: the astrality that comes from above and identifies with itself becomes through this act a non-communicative or senseless form.[18] It is like a caricature of the true I (Chapter I.6) that awakens through the self-experience of the form-free attentiveness.[19] At the same time, it is the kernel of egotism (Appendix 10).

V.4. Astrality and the Etheric

The astral and the etheric are *downward* metamorphoses of the spiritual being, enabling it to link itself to the lower human form. As seen from below, the physical body becomes alive and capable of feeling through these entities, so that the connection to the higher human can take place. We can observe how the sentient body (also called the soul body or, in a narrow sense, the astral body) directs the life of the organism through the life body. It is the vegetative nervous system that represents the presence of this sentient body in the organism.

If consciousness were to awaken within the astral, that is, if we had an astral awareness, we would perceive the etheric. In other words: the awareness of the etheric (that is, not only the life body, but also the life forces that become free and then those that lose their freedom) lies in the astral. The free life forces are forces of thinking and mental imagery, not specific thoughts and mental images; they are, as capacities, above and outside normal awareness—superconscious. Meditation at its lowest level is often referred to by Steiner as "soul behavior with the power of thought."[20] We work, not so much with thoughts (though these may serve as a starting point), but with the form-free power of thinking. The etheric *body*, by contrast, consists in living, formed life-forces; these forms are responsible for the form-driven growth of the organism and for keeping it alive.

The relationship of the etheric and astral is described in the little book, *The Threshold of the Spiritual World*, (CW 17), in the chapter "Remarks" (Appendix 11). If experiences are described "objectively," they can be presented as elemental (etheric) processes. If they are described *as experiences*, then the same events can be described as occurring in the world of the soul (Appendix 12).

Just as the psychosomatic mechanism (through the sentient body and through the I-body as well) is guided by the organism's sensitivity, the free life-forces are led by cognitive feeling: by the feeling of logic, or evidence (Appendix 13). In both cases, the way our liveliness works has to do with feeling. This is what makes it possible to describe the same processes in the two styles just outlined. On the one hand, we can describe the life-event (etheric event), and on the other we can describe how the same event is grasped through feeling—an astral event.

In his lecture cycles on the Gospels, Rudolf Steiner speaks repeatedly about the Lord's healings (Appendix 14). The anthropological distinction between human beings at the time of Jesus and those of our time consists principally in this: earlier, the etheric was not co-extensive with the physical but "rather reached out beyond the physical body on all sides," while in our time "the etheric body has descended most deeply into the physical." This relationship determines the possibility of soul-spiritual healing: in the first case, it is relatively accessible; in the second it is very limited. (Of course, we have to take into account what was cited in Appendix 1, that these expressions are all symbolic or imagistic and have nothing to do with space—just as in our description of a "separating robe").

The etheric that "reaches out beyond the physical" consists in free life-forces, which link the human being upward, toward our spiritual, superconscious parts. Through the astral "robe" that develops, the I-body, these free life-forces are forced into the "physical body"— that is, into the robe or the I-body. They become woven into it, formed, and so lose their connection to what is above, and also to the possibility of healing. According to Steiner (Appendix 14), we are "close to the boundary point where the etheric body will emerge once more, make itself free of the physical body, and become more independent; and as humanity rushes toward the future, the etheric body will emerge more and more from out of the physical body.... In a certain sense [soul-spiritual healing] will become possible again, for we are, after all, approaching that future time in which the spirit will regain its significance." The phenomena of psychosomatics and the influence of the soul-spiritual on bodily illnesses are increasing at a very fast pace.

Summary

In the healings, the separating robe was lifted for a moment; the life forces were freed. In this way, a link between the higher and lower human being was established. The signs of this process are given in sentences such as "thy sins are forgiven," or "thy faith hath saved thee." This faith is not only the unshakeable certainty that the healing will take place, but also the paradisial primal certainty that humanity lives in a meaningful, Logos-created world that is guided by God. Sometimes the I-power of the Logos is emphasized, as in the words, "I say unto you, I will." The trapped life-forces and forces of feeling are released. This gives rise to a structure in which the true I, awakened by the Savior's presence, can work on the physical body through the higher astrality and through the free life-forces from above and from below. What happens then is similar to the formation of the body through the formative forces after conception, or in the child's growth after birth.

Meditation

To become whole (healthy) is to *grow* healthy.

APPENDICES

All citations, unless otherwise noted, are from the Collected Works of Rudolf Steiner (CW) and are translated directly from the German editions (Gesamtausgabe).

Appendix 1: CW 17, *The Threshold of the Spiritual World*, Afterword, 1918:

There are people who are actually disappointed when the spiritual researcher has to tell them that when he speaks in terms taken from sensory experience, he means only to make accessible what he has beheld. For such people do not really strive to know a supersensible world distinct from the sensory; rather, they want to find a kind of double of the sensory world as the supersensible. This supersensible world is supposed to be more delicate, "more etheric," than the sensory world; but apart from that they don't want it to require us to understand it differently from the sensory. But anyone who truly wants to approach the spiritual world has to get comfortable with the task of acquiring new ideas. If you only want to imagine a diluted, cloudy copy of the sensory world, you will never grasp the supersensible.

Appendix 2: CW 93a, October 16, 1905

When we consider human development, we find that one part of the astral body is continually trying to overcome the other, lower half, and vice versa.... In the etheric body, too, there are two parts that continually try each to overcome the other.... When a human being dies, the etheric body splits into two parts. One comes from our higher development, and this is the part we take with us. The whole rest of the etheric body falls away, for the human being can exercise no mastery over it; it came to him from the outside. He can only master it by becoming a student of spiritual science.....The etheric body consists of two members: the part of human nature that came over from the Moon and then its opposite pole.... The one is the pole of animality; the other is the spiritual, the mental body. In between is the astral body, which also arose from the connection of two parts.... The higher nature is originally connected with the mental body.... One quality of the lower astral body is that it has desires. The upper portion has instead devotion, love, the gift of generosity....

Appendix 3: CW 226, May 16, 1923

In reality, even while awake by day we remain, as far as our I and astral body go, in the state we enjoyed during our pre-earthly existence. We have to accustom ourselves to the idea that the I and the astral body don't actually participate in our earthly development. They remain fundamentally behind: they stay where they are, while we make ourselves ready to receive physical and etheric bodies. So even during waking life, our I and astral body remain at the point of the initiation of our earthly life.... But in the I we talk about every day, we don't have our real I at all. Instead, our real I stands at the initial instant of our earthly life. Our physical body mirrors back the mirror-image of our true I, through the etheric body's mediation, according to every moment when the physical body is alive. This mirror image of the true I, which we receive back from our physical body at every moment, really does come from something that never went along with earthly existence. And we call this mirror image our I…. And it is the etheric body that extends out of the present moment, as if in perspective, toward our true I and toward our astral body, which do not come down into the physical world at all.

CW 228, September 2, 1923:

We really do not take our actual, true, inner I out of the spiritual world and into this physical world. We always leave it within the spiritual world…. When, by day, we have our contemporary consciousness as human beings and call ourselves "I," this word is an indication of something that isn't actually present in this physical world, but only has its image in the physical world.
(See also the entirety of booklet CW 17, as well as CW 66, 2 March, 1917; CW 141, 7 January, 1913).

Appendix 4: CW 96, October 22, 1906

There is no firm boundary between the etheric and the astral body.

Appendix 5: CW 107, November 2, 1908

[For human beings], apart from the section of the etheric body used for growth and thus enclosed within certain bounds for the sake of this development, there is something like another part of the etheric body that is free, that has no pre-ordained usage—unless, through education, we introduce all kinds of things into the soul that this free part of the etheric body can then process. So there really is, in the human being, a part of the etheric body that isn't used by nature.

Appendix 6: Rainer Maria Rilke,

"Initiale":

From infinite yearnings arise
finite deeds, like weak fountains,
that tremble and bend over too soon.
But our glad powers, which otherwise
keep silent from us,
are revealed in these dancing tears.

Appendix 7: CW 303, December 29, 1921

And it is of particular importance precisely for the child in these first two and one half years of life, that it is not accessible to a foreign will, but instead has a fine, instinctive capacity to perceive everything that happens around it, in particular in the people who surround it, especially those who raise it, and with whom the child has a certain rapport of the soul. It is not as if the outward gaze were particularly honed; it is not a question of a definite seeing, but rather a total perception of the most intimate kind, oriented to what is happening in the outer world around the child—and which is not taking place with the express intention of having an influence on the child.... But from this it follows that we have to take into account this receptivity, which still contains perception completely embedded within feeling (See also Appendix 10).

Appendix 8: CW 231, November 16, 1923

Certainly, if we remain here in the physical and sensory earthly life, we see all too often how little success is enjoyed by what springs from the best moral impulses, while much that does not come from good moral impulses has great success. Why is this? It is this way because the physical-sensory world, which we have "attracted" in a certain way—for we have taken on a piece of it as the robe of our body—does not, after all, contain moral impulses.

Appendix 9: CW 187, December 27, 1918

...the real I comes to a stop when we are born. What we experience as our I is the mirror image of the I. It is only something that mirrors the pre-birth I....we only experience something of the real I quite indirectly. What psychologists speak of as the I is only a mirror image.

CW 17, Chapter V

To the extent that the elementary and sensory worlds are only mirrors of the spiritual, the etheric and physical-sensory human body also have to be considered mirrorings of the astral human nature.... As the later aphorisms in this work will show, even the I that we address in normal life as our own being is not the "true I," but the mirror image of the "true I" in the physical-sensory world. From an etheric point of view, the etheric mirroring of the astral body can become an illusion of the "true astral body."

Appendix 10: CW 156, October 5, 1914

There is something here in the human soul that, on the one hand, can transform itself into all other humans and beings, and that, on the other hand, can develop into egotism. We must be able to carry this understanding into the Cosmos if we wish to acquire spiritual hearing.

Appendix 11: CW 17, Remarks

From theosophy and spiritual science, we realize that soon after the separation of the physical-sensory body from the soul at death, that portion of the body is also dissolved which we have called "etheric" in this text. Afterward, the soul then lives in the entity that has been designated here as the astral body. The etheric body transforms itself, after its dissolution from the soul, within the elementary world. It enters into those beings who make up the elementary world. The soul of the human being is no longer present during this transformation of the etheric body. But the soul does, after death, experience the processes of this elemental world *as its outer world*. This experience of the elemental world *from without* is portrayed in theosophy and in spiritual science as the progress of the soul through the soul-world. We have to imagine, then, that this soul world is the same as what we describe here, from the standpoint of supersensible consciousness, as the elemental world. (See the entire chapter of "Notes.")

Appendix 12: For example: CW 107, February 15, 1909. [Re: Christ in the astral (normally called the etheric) sphere]:

This entity, which only came into connection with our earth in the beginning of our current time-reckoning, was incarnate for three years in a body of flesh, and has stood in connection with the astral sphere of our supersensible world since then. This being, as an avatar, is of completely unique significance. The simple Saxon curate who wrote the poem ["Savior"] had, from immediate clairvoyant sight, the certainty that Christ is present on the astral plane.

Appendix 13: CW 59, October 28, 1909

Logical thinking cannot itself be proved through logical thinking, but only through feeling, through the feeling for truth, incapable of error, to be found within the human soul. So from this classical example we see that logic itself has feeling as its basis; feeling underlies thinking.

Appendix 14: CW 123, September 9, 1910

However much it may be doubted today, right up to the time of Christ healing processes could be carried out by making a person clairvoyant. Today, when human beings have sunk more deeply into the physical plane, this is no longer possible. At that time the soul was still easier to affect, so that through certain processes it could be made clairvoyant and able to live its way into the spiritual world. And since the spiritual world sends a healthy and health-making force all the way into the physical world, this introduced the possibility of healing.

CW 123, September 10, 1910

The power of the soul, the power of the spirit, had a much

greater, immediate impact on the human body than it did later on when the body became denser.... Therefore, it was far more possible at that time to heal from out of the soul. They [the healers] cleansed the soul and permeated it with healthy sensations, impulses, and forces of will through soul/spiritual influences that they could practice, whether in the normal state of physical perception or in the so-called temple sleep, which was nothing other at that time than a way of putting the person in a state of clairvoyance.... So someone speaking in terms of that time would have said: There are people who have access to the mysteries who, through sacrifice of their own I-consciousness, can put themselves in touch with certain soul-spiritual forces that then radiate out to the environment, so that they become healers for this environment.... But what is most significant about this is that the author of the Gospel of Matthew recounts: Here is a person who has brought a new essential power into humanity, who has carried out healings through the power of his own I, out of which it was not previously possible to heal; he introduced the very power with which, beforehand, it was not possible to heal.

CW 114, September 24, 1909

At this time [ancient Indian culture], when the etheric body still extended far beyond the physical on all sides, and was less densely connected with it than is the case today, forces and qualities of the human soul still had a far greater power over the physical body. But the more the etheric body drove its way into the physical, the weaker it became, and the less power it had over the physical body.... In our time, the etheric body has sunk down the most deeply ever into the physical body, and is most tied to the facts of the physical body. We are close to the final limit, when the etheric body will emerge again, make itself free from the physical body, and become more independent. And as humanity rushes toward the future, the etheric body will come out of the physical more and more.... In the [ancient] Indian body, the etheric body is still relatively free, and the soul can develop forces that have an effect on the physical body. The etheric body receives the forces of the soul because it is still not so bound to the physical body; instead, it controls the physical body all the more, and the result is that what was done to the soul at that time had a tremendous effect on the body.... Today it is not possible to have such an immediate effect on the human soul so that it really penetrates through to the whole physical organization. It is not possible in a direct way. But it will become possible, because we are nearing that future in which the spiritual will regain its full significance.

NOTES

1. Compare M. Merleau-Ponty, *The Primacy of Percep-
    tion* (Northwestern University Press, 1964):
    "...The perception of others is made comprehen-
    sible if one supposes that psychogenesis begins in
    a state when the child is unaware of himself and
    the other as different beings. We cannot say that in
    such a state the child has a genuine communication
    with others. In order that there be communication,
    there must be a sharp distinction between one who
    communicates and the one with whom he commu-
    nicates. But there is initially a state of pre-communi-
    cation (Max Scheler), wherein the others' intentions
    somehow play across my body while my intentions
    play across his.... there is first a phase which we call
    pre-communication, in which there is not one indi-
    vidual over against another but rather an anony-
    mous collectivity, an undifferentiated group life (*vie
    a plusieurs*).... To tell the truth, it seems that the
    first forms of reaction to others described by Guil-
    laume (*L'imitation chez l'enfant* Paris, 1925) are not
    connected with a visual perception of others; they
    correspond, rather, to the date of introceptivity...."

What is termed "precommunication" here is the signless, direct communication; all the other traits of early childhood are also mentioned.

2. Rudolf Steiner on the I-body:

CW 16, VI Meditation:
"The tapestry of memories, which one now regards as his earlier 'I,'" can also be called the I-body or the thought-body."

CW 34, *The Education of the Child*:
"The bearer of the capacity mentioned here [to call oneself "I"], is the 'I-body', the fourth member of the human being."

CW 60, November 10, 1910:
"But in the human being we can say that this astral body is still permeated by an I-body."

CW 96, October 19, 1906:
"When three further planets have been passed through, then the I-body of the human being will be as far advanced as the physical body is today.

CW 283, November 26, 1906:
Something very different is meant by "I-body" here — an example of the lack of a consistent terminology.

3. Kühlewind, *Star Children*, Rudolf Steiner Press 2004; H. Köhler, *War Michel aus Loenneberg Aufmerksamkeit-gestoert?* V.Fr.G. 2002; *Was haben wir nur falsch gemacht?* V.Fr.G. 2000.

4. Kühlewind, *Attention and Devotion*, V.Fr.G. 1998, Chapters 13 and 18.

5. Son (or sons) of the light: Luke 16:8; John 12:36; Ephesians 5:8; 1 Thessalonians 5:5. "Son" most often designates one who can testify about the "Father," so the "Son of God" can testify about God.

6. *The Zen Teaching of Bodhidharma*, "Bloodstream Sermon," North Point Press 1989.

7. Kühlewind, *The Renewal of the Holy Spirit*, V.Fr.G. 1992, "Baptism."

8. Kühlewind, *The Soft Will*, V.Fr.G. 2000, Chapter III.

9. Ibid., Exercises 35 and 36.

10. See note 4.

11. *The Soft Will*, Chapter I, exercises 7, 8, and 9.

12. Kühlewind, *From Normal to Healthy*, Anthroposophic Press 1988, Chapter 3.4; "Attention and Devotion," Chapter 18.

13. *Eudokia* here means *right understanding*, see Kühlewind, *Christmas*, V.Fr.G. 1999, the Chapter "Peace on Earth."

14. For "house" see Kühlewind, *Becoming Aware of the Logos*, Chapter 8.

15. For "unhiddenness" see *Becoming Aware of the Logos*, Chapter 10 and Kühlewind, *The Kingdom of God*, V.Fr.G. 1994, Chapter "Unhiddenness."

16. See *Becoming Aware of the Logos*, Chapter 5.

17. See *The Renewal of the Holy Spirit*, Chapters "Languages and Language" and "Healing and Pentecostal Speech."

18. See *Attention and Devotion*, Chapters 6-8.

19. *The Soft Will*, Exercises 9 and 17; "Remarks," p. 80.

20. CW 138, October 28, 1912: *The Guardian of the Threshold*, VIII; CW 271, May 5, 1918.

Regarding spiritual experience:

"Feeling and willing develop in such a way that they appear before the human soul as objective entities with the power of thought, while the remainder of perceiving and imaging, which would otherwise remain unnoticed within feeling and willing, is revealed as capable of placing itself within the spiritual world."

Further Reading

(Available from Lindisfarne Books / SteinerBooks —
www. Steinerbooks.org or SteinerBooks PO Box 960
Herndon, VA 20172-0960. Phone (703) 661-1594.
FAX (703) 661-1501)—and through all bookstores)

By Georg Kühlewind:

Stages of Consciousness: Meditations on the Boundaries of the Soul.

Becoming Aware of the Logos: The Way of St. John the Evangelist

From Normal to Healthy: Paths to the Liberation of Consciousness

The Life of the Soul: Between Subconsciousness and Supraconsciousnes

The Logos-Structure of the World: Language As Model of Reality

Working with Anthroposophy: The Practice of Thinking

Star Children: Understanding Children Who Set Us Special Tasks and Challenge

The Light of the "I": Guidelines for Meditation

By Rudolf Steiner:

Truth and Science

Intuitive Thinking as a Spiritual Path

How to Know Higher Worlds

Theosophy

An Outline of Esoteric Science

A Way of Self-Knowledge and The Threshold of the Spiritual World

By Michael Lipson:

Stairway of Surprise

By Massimo Scaligero:

The Light

(Available from Rudolf Steiner College Press, 9200 Fair Oaks Blvd., Fair Oaks, CA. Phone (916) 961-8727. Fax (916) 961-8731. www.steinercollege.edu.)

By Georg Kühlewind:

Schooling of Consciousness: Selected Essays
(Ed. Friedemann Schwarzkopf)

Thinking of the Heart and Other Essays
(Ed. Friedemann Schwarzkopf)